Amazing Grace

By
Charles Hodge

Amazing Grace

By
Charles Hodge

Amazing Grace

Amazing grace! How Sweet the sound
That saved a wretch like me!
I once was lost, but now am found;
Was blind, but now I see.

'Twas grace that taught my heart to fear,
And grace my fears relieved.
How precious did that grace appear
The hour I first believed!

Thru many dangers, trials, and snares
I have already come.
'Tis grace hath brought me safe thus far,
And grace will lead me home.

When we've been there ten thousand years,
Bright, shining as the sun,
We've no less days to sing God's praise
Than when we first begun.

                              John Newton

Contents

LESSON 1

Amazing Grace

Introduction

AMAZING GRACE! Sing it! Preach it! Live it! Tell men what God did before you tell men what to do. Christianity began, continues, and ends in grace. Everything ultimately depends upon God's grace. Christianity stands or falls upon grace. The central and distinctive feature of the Gospel is grace. "But by the grace of God I am what I am: and his grace which was bestowed upon me was not in vain: but I laboured more abundantly than they all: yet not I, but the grace of God which was with me" (1 Cor. 15:10). The only permanent motivation in Christianity is grace. "For the love of Christ constraineth us" (2 Cor. 5:14). It is not our love for God but His love for us that motivates. When you awaken each morning remind yourself that God loves you and Jesus died for you. This is your Christian motivation. Sinners artificially got must be artificially kept. The cross saves; the Gospel is "Good News." Bring sinners to the cross; keep Christians at the cross. Never turn the "Good News" into "Bad News." Christianity is not "Right answers to selected questions"; Christianity is not performance oriented; Christianity is not one's ability to pass a religious quiz at the judgment. Man cannot save himself by himself. He cannot know enough, do enough, live enough to merit salvation. Sinners are not only in the hands of an angry God—they are in the hands of a loving God! "If so be ye have tasted that the Lord is gracious" (1 Pet. 2:3). "We love him, because he first loved us" (1 Jn. 4:11). "And he said unto me, my grace is sufficient for thee: for my strength is made perfect in weakness" (2 Cor. 12:9). Grace is the warp and the woof of the Christian's entire relationship to God. "For God

1

so loved the world, that he gave his only begotten Son, that whosoever believeth in him should not perish, but have everlasting life'' (Jn. 3:16). We are saved by grace—don't you ever forget it!

Saved By Grace

Salvation by grace is *THE* basic Biblical doctrine! Christianity is a grace religion. Karl Barth was asked to name the most profound thought in the universe. His answer, "Jesus loves me, this I know." "For by grace are ye saved through faith; and that not of yourselves: it is the gift of God: not of works, lest any man should boast" (Eph. 2:8,9). "To the praise of the glory of his grace, wherein he hath made us accepted in the beloved. In whom we have redemption through his blood, the forgiveness of sins, according to the riches of his grace" (Eph. 1:6,7). "Being justified freely by his grace through the redemption that is in Christ Jesus (Rom. 3:24). "For the wages of sin is death; but the gift of God is eternal life through Jesus Christ our Lord" (Rom. 6:23). "Moreover the law entered, that the offense might abound. But where sin abounded, grace did much more abound: That as sin hath reigned unto death even so might grace reign through righteousness unto eternal life by Jesus Christ our Lord" (Rom. 5:19,20). If any sinner is saved it will be by the grace of God! "For I am not ashamed of the gospel of Christ: for it is the power of God unto salvation to every one that believeth; to the Jew first, and also to the Greek" (Rom. 1:16).

Charis — Charis — Charis

"But none of these things move me, neither count I my life dear unto myself, so that I might finish my course with joy, and the ministry, which I have received of the Lord Jesus, to testify the gospel of the grace of God" (Acts 20:24). The Greek word for grace is charis, chara (rejoice), charisma. In classical Greek the word means beautiful, lovely, attractive, charming—that which is delightful. It also, from Latin, includes gratitude.

The result is graciousness. *TREAT PEOPLE RIGHT!* The Christian life is the gracious life. People that receive grace give mercy. One's mercy problem is always a grace problem (Mt. 9:11-13). Grace also produces generosity (2 Cor. 8). The Macedonian liberality came from the soil of grace. The grace of God does not call us out of misery into more misery nor out of gloom into more gloom. "Now our Lord Jesus Christ himself, and God, even our Father, which hath loved us, and hath given us everlasting consolation and good hope through grace" (2 Thess. 2:16). Grace, charis, is one beautiful word. Learn to say it without mumbling!

But the highest usage of charis is the cross of Christ! What God did for man in sin at Calvary! Charis is the unmerited, undeserved, unconditional love of God. Grace is what every sinner needs but none deserve. "But God commendeth his love toward us, in that, while we were yet sinners, Christ died for us" (Rom. 5:8).

> Justice—We get what we deserve.
> Mercy—We do not get what we deserve.
> Grace—We get what we do not deserve.

Grace is the surprise of the Gospel accounts! The miracle of miracles. What we dare not think, cannot understand, has happened! God, our enemy, the slayer of our gods, our justifiable accuser, has become our Friend, our affirmer, our vindicator. Grace is positive acceptance in spite of the other person; a demonstration of love that is unearned, undeserved, and unrepayable. Unconditional love is hard to grasp; it is even more difficult to communicate. "I love you . . . I love you as you are . . . I love you unconditionally." Grace is the unilateral character of God's righteousness. *GRACE— GRACE—GRACE!*

> The love of God is broader
> Than the measure of man's mind.
> And the heart of the Eternal
> Is most wonderfully kind.

Grace, then, is a gift which implies the presence of the giver. The giver and gift are so involved the gift cannot be handed over unless the giver is involved. Grace involves (1) need in

3

the recipient and (2) power to meet that need in the giver. This makes grace also practical. Water would be of no value to a drowning man! Grace is the gift the man needs! Yet this also exposes the paradox of grace. Grace contradicts the world and our own strength (2 Cor. 1:12; 10:13; 12:9), and establishes a beachhead for a new life! Grace always shatters the calculations of legalism and comes to us in a great surprise! Grace is the atmosphere in which Christians live. "But the God of all grace, who hath called us into his eternal glory by Christ Jesus, after that ye have suffered a while, make you perfect, establish, strengthen, settle you" (1 Pet. 5:10). "Unconditional, spontaneous, unmerited, never-ending love of God." *GRACE!* Shout it from the house-tops!

Charis is in the New Testament 170 times. 101 times by Paul. Never by Jesus as He was grace, "For the law was given by Moses, but grace and truth came by Jesus Christ" (Jn. 1:17).

Not A Business Transaction

This is the temptation of flawed humanity. To reduce salvation to a business transaction. Consciously or unconsciously man is always balancing the books, earning salvation, deserving to be saved. Man refuses to admit that all are on charity (grace). "For all have sinned, and come short of the glory of God" (Rom. 3:23,10). God did not pay 50¢ with man equally paying 50¢. This is hard for man's pride to swallow! It is not even 90¢ from God and 10¢ from man! *JESUS PAID IT ALL!* 100¢ on the dollar! This is grace.

Salvation is atonement not attainment! It is from believing not achieving. Man is spiritually bankrupt! He cannot even pay the interest let alone the principal! *PRAISE GOD!* We are free from "Bootstrap Religion," a "Do-It-Yourself Salvation." God did not merely drop the Bible out of the sky saying, "Good Luck"! People that are trying to balance their "Spiritual Books" can only proselyte others to self-righteousness. Men convert others to who they are. This frees men from a performance mentality with the wishful thought, "I hope the Lord returns on one of my good days!" Jesus said,

4

".. for I am not come to call the righteous, but sinners to repentance" (Mt. 9:13), "... Verily, I say unto you, that the publicans and the harlots go into the kingdom of God before you" (Mt. 21:13). Sinners can understand sin and appreciate grace. As someone said, "The Church is not a hotel for saints but a hospital for sinners."

If grace is not for sinners it is not grace; if mercy is not for the undeserving it is not mercy (Rom. 9:15). Since salvation is the free gift of God there is nothing that man can do to achieve, merit, or earn it. Unmerited favor cannot be merited! God did what we could not do! Jesus paid what we could not pay! From beginning to the end it is all of grace and none of man's merits! This is hard for man to swallow! The entire scheme of redemption, including all that God has done, is doing, and will do, is one continuous act of grace. Salvation was planned and executed before sinners were told about it. Grace is "free gratis." God justifies the ungodly. "To wit, that God was in Christ, reconciling the world unto himself, not imputing their trespasses unto them; and hath committed unto us the word of reconciliation . . . For he hath made him to be sin for us, who knew no sin; that we might be made the righteousness of God in him" (2 Cor. 5:19-21). "Forasmuch as ye know that ye were not redeemed with corruptible things, as silver and gold, from your vain conversation received by tradition from your fathers; but with the precious blood of Christ, as of a lamb without blemish and without spot" (1 Pet. 1:18,19). "Who his own self bore our sins in his body on the tree, that we, being dead to sins, should live unto righteousness: by whose stripes ye were healed" (1 Pet. 2:24). God is the "Eternal Short" for good!

Grace Is Not Dangerous

The truth about grace cannot be dangerous! Universalism is wrong! License is wrong! "Cheap grace" is wrong! Why are we afraid of grace? Why must grace always be explained? Can one know too much about God? Can one overly-emphasize the cross? Is Christ dangerous? Can God receive too much glory? Is obedience dangerous? Must works always be explained? Is baptism to be feared? Why, in a 45 minute sermon, must one preach grace for 5 minutes then take 40 minutes to allow works? Is this ever reversed? Are we focusing upon God's grace or man's performance? Do we enjoy sermons on baptism more than sermons on the cross? Do we preach guilt without grace? Because sectarians preach grace does that make grace wrong? Does this mean it should not be foundational?

> I owed a debt I could not pay
> He paid a debt He did not owe
> I needed someone to wash my sins away.
> So now I sing a brand-new song—
> "Amazing Grace"
> Christ Jesus paid the debt I could never pay.

Christianity is not merely a "spruced-up Law of Moses." Christianity is a grace-faith system as opposed to law-works. This is our faith and hope. Some neither want the grace of God nor the God of grace. They have reduced Christianity to what they know and do. Christianity, to them, is but another burden! Grace can understand works, but works has no place for grace. Grace cannot be explained by law. There cannot be any gospel to the self-righteous (1 Tim. 1:11-17). Grace is not "too good to be true"—it is "too good not to be true." Legalist brethren always stumble over the depths of the grace of God. Legalism demands that you qualify! Grace that can be qualified for has ceased to be grace! It is like one before his banker seeking a loan. He has to prove that financially he does not need it before he can receive it! As a wit observed, "Grace is a wonderful thing in the Church of Christ until you need it!" Frightening, isn't it? The apostle Paul never got over salvation by grace! We can be wrong about many things but we cannot be wrong about grace!

Preach The Gospel Of Grace

The Gospel is the good news of grace. "But though we, or an angel from heaven, preach any other gospel unto you than that which we have preached unto you, let him be accursed"

6

(Gal. 1:6-10). Familiar scriptures must be read more closely. They usually don't teach what we think they do. Paul is not saying, "Be right on all the issues" . . . "The Crisis of the Year." Paul is telling the Galatians who received grace not to return to law! They were trying to make grace law! It cannot be done. Paul is telling them to emphasize grace not perfection—what God did not, what man does. Sermons, lessons, that fail to emphasize grace is not Gospel! It is that plain and simple! This is a perverted Gospel. If you obey any command with a sense of self-pride rather than from a trust in Christ you have perverted the Gospel! You have denied the saving power of the cross! God's greatest glory is in man's utter hopelessness.

O Lord, give me grace to feel the need of Thy grace
Give me grace to ask for thy grace
And when in Thy grace Thou hast given me
    GRACE—give me the grace to use Thy grace.
                                    Duchess of Gordon

Questions

1. Discuss attitudes toward grace in the class members and brotherhood before serious studies of grace begin.
2. Do *YOU* believe in grace? emphasize grace? study grace? Are you growing in grace?
3. Do you feel more comfortable with law/works? Does grace bother you?
4. Discuss the Greek word, charis, in detail.
5. Discuss the vital relation between the "Giver and the Gift."
6. Have we reduced salvation to a business transaction? Do we try "to earn it"?
7. Is grace dangerous? Are works dangerous?
8. Explain Galatians 1:6-10.

LESSON 2

The Demands Of Grace

Introduction

AMAZING GRACE! Shout it from the housetops! Get on your knees in praise and thank God for it. Tell men what God did before you tell men what to do. Jesus bought what I could not buy; He did what I could not do. There is no sin too strong for the blood to cleanse; there is no sinner too evil for Christ to forgive; there is no Christian too good for Christ to make better. To God be the glory!

With many the New Testament begins with Acts; the Epistles are the focus. But the New Testament begins with Matthew, Mark, Luke, and John (MMLJ)! The Gospel accounts. These four books reveal Christ. The difference in the first century was Christ; the difference in the twentieth century will be Christ. *CHRIST—CHRIST—CHRIST!* You do not reap Acts by planting Acts! You reap Acts by planting MMLJ! The failure is not in Acts! The power to live the epistles is found in MMLJ! In the book of Acts Christ was preached and the church resulted—without exception. You cannot preach "The Church" and result with Christ! God's method is a *MESSAGE*—Christ!

Acts 2:42 is a "Hall of Fame" verse, "And they continued stedfastly in the apostles' doctrine, and fellowship, and in breaking of bread, and in prayers." What is apostolic doctrine? Apostolic doctrine does not refer to the epistles—they were written years later. Apostolic doctrine is not "Church Organization." None existed until Acts 6. Elders were not revealed until Acts 11. What is apostolic doctrine? Again, what were the apostles uniquely qualified and prepared to do? To reveal Christ! "And he ordained twelve, that they should be

9

with him (Mk. 3:14). "... they marvelled; and they took knowledge of them, that they had been with Jesus" (Acts 4:13). Read the sermon of Peter in Acts 2—outline all the sermons in Acts. They are all the same—*CHRIST!* Men were told what God did! They cried aloud in response. What did the new converts need? *CHRIST* (Mt. 28:18-20)! The apostles taught Christ (Acts 5:42). Jerusalem was filled with apostolic doctrine (Acts 5:28). Jerusalem was filled with *CHRIST!* We must return to *"CHRIST"* preaching! There can be many scriptures yet no *CHRIST!* The only permanent motivation in Christianity is the grace of God. We are saved by grace; don't you ever forget it!

> I cannot work my soul to save,
> That work my Lord has done,
> But I will work like any slave,
> For the love of God's dear Son.

God's Grace Is Free

"Thanks be unto God for his unspeakable gift" (2 Cor. 9:15). "... but the gift of God is eternal life through Jesus Christ our Lord (Rom. 6:23). "Being justified by his grace through the redemption that is in Christ Jesus" (Rom. 3:24). "Now to him that worketh is the reward not reckoned of grace, but of debt" (Rom. 4:4). "Therefore it is of faith, that it might be by grace" (Rom. 4:16). "And if by grace, then is it no more of works: otherwise grace is no more grace. But if it be of works, then is it no more grace: otherwise work is no more work" (Rom. 11:6).

Yet what men need they resist, yea fight and hate? *WHY?* (1) Because grace renders man totally helpless, dependent. Man wishes success, sufficiency, achievement. Grace says man is religiously bankrupt. Grace eliminates salvation from being a business transaction. Jesus paid it all. A friend comes by in his car, takes you out to an expensive restaurant and buys you the best steak. All is enjoyed, *BUT* you demand your right to give the tip! This is the pride of man! Religiously in Christ, you cannot even pay for the tip! Grace is something you can

10

never buy—it is only given! We are all on charity! One cannot earn it, deserve it, or bring it about! Grace frees man from self-effort. Grace is not "Bootstrap Religion." Christianity is not a "self-improvement" course. God did not drop the Bible out of the sky with a note attached, "Good Luck." Grace contradicts "Deism." The Jews stumbled over the cross because it cut away the taproot of arrogance in self-justification! Man refuses to be baptized, "Until I know I can hold out." How silly! Defeated, frustrated Christians are all over our land suffering from the "Creed of Self-Reliance." We have just about promoted ourselves to death! We have preached guilt but not grace. We have preached works but not grace. The legalistic mind cannot grasp the depths of the grace of God! Grace, given, must be accepted! Sin was pride at its ultimate; grace forces humility to its ultimate.

> Nothing in my hand I bring
> Helpless to Thy cross I cling
> Naked came to Thee for dress,
> Helpless come to Thee for grace,
> Vile I to the fountain fly,
> Wash me, Savior, or I die.

(2) Man fears grace because he concludes grace eliminates obedience (human responsibility). Man is funny. The law was given to totally expose the fact man could not keep it. Yet man wants law, rules, regulations. One can preach an entire sermon on obedience without mentioning grace. But one had better not even so much as make one point on grace without explaining obedience! *QUIZ TIME!* Do we love Mk. 16:15,16 more than John 3:16? Are we more careful about what a sinner knows specifically about baptism than what he knows generally about grace? Can we literally argue one into the baptistry without converting him to Christ? Grace does not eliminate human responsibility—grace *EMPHASIZES* human responsibility! When man gets the cross the cross gets him! This is the "Power Paradox" of grace! Universalism is wrong, totally wrong. *ANY MAN, ANYWHERE, AT ANY TIME CAN GO TO HELL!* Irresistible grace is not only anti-scriptural it is downright silly! Man is the only creation that can choose. A dog is a dog is a dog. Man chooses; man is a free moral agent.

11

Man can respond to the amazing grace of God. Grace is not dangerous! The more grace one grasps the more obedient one will be. Christianity is *INTAKE* not *OUTPUT!* The more Christ one has the more active one will be. Grace does not make one irresponsible; grace makes one responsible. "What shall we say then? Shall we continue in sin, that grace may abound? God forbid" (Rom. 6:1,2). Human responsibility is outlawed when thinking that man can save himself by himself. "Do your best and God will do the rest" is blasphemy! Our righteousness is as "filthy rags" (Isa. 64:6). No man can merit salvation (Rom. 3:10). Human responsibility means responding to, accepting, appropriating the grace of God. Consequently one does not obey the law, works—one obeys the Gospel (Mk. 16:15, 16; 2 Thess. 1:7-9; 1 Pet. 4:16-18). No one can take responsibility for you, your life, and your actions. Acceptance of grace is up to you.

Grace does not stand against good works. Its antithesis is not good works but merit. Grace creates good works; grace demands obedience. Ruling out works does not rule out obedience.

Grace That Is Free Is Not Cheap

"Cheap Grace" is not grace. The grace of God cost heaven its finest jewel—the Son of God! There is no price as grace! Christianity is not some cheap escape from the way things are. The death of Jesus is His final and total commitment to us. "And I, if I be lifted up from the earth, will draw all men unto me. This he said, signifying what death he should die" (Jn. 12:32,33). "No man can come to me, except the Father which hath sent me draw him: and I will raise him up at the last day" (Jn. 6:44). Christianity is free yet it is costly. ". . . If any man will come after me, let him deny himself, and take up his cross, and follow me" (Mt. 16:24). "I am crucified with Christ: nevertheless I live; yet not I, but Christ liveth in me . . . I do not frustrate the grace of God" (Gal. 2:20,21).

Grace is not merely a gift of principle; it is a gift of obligation! It would be a disgrace not to accept grace: "We then beseech you also that ye receive not the grace of God in vain" (2 Cor. 6:1).

Love so amazing, so divine,
Demands my soul, my life, my all.

No law can legislate or demand equal with love! How dare
any man reject the cross of Christ! Grace delivers agonizing
responsibilities, duties, and obligations. Paul said, "For though
I preach the gospel I have nothing to glory of: for necessity
is laid upon me; yea, woe is unto me, if I preach not the
gospel!" (1 Cor. 9:16). We were chosen by grace to choose
grace! Someone said, "Grace drives me to God to keep me
from forgetting what I owe Him." Salvation is rooted in the
grace of God. Preach grace! Never fear grace!

Grace Causes Repentance

Most believe that repentance is caused by the badness of
man. This can only be temporary. Man may find relief or cause
some reformation. But only grace (the goodness of God) can
cause genuine repentance. "Or despiseth thou the riches of his
goodness and forbearance and longsuffering; not knowing that
the goodness of God leadeth thee to repentance?" (Rom. 2:4).
"For godly sorrow worketh repentance to salvation not to be
repented of: but the sorrow of the world worketh death" (2
Cor. 7:10). God did not center His power in creation, at the
flood, in the exodus—God centered *ALL* His power at the
cross! Grace reveals the awesome power of the cross.
   The greatest demonstration is in Luke 15. Read verse 18,19
then verse 21, then verse 20. What is the difference in verses
18,19, then 21? One little phrase, "make me as one of thy hired
servants." The Prodigal had but "rock bottom." Logically,
he had "come to himself." But even upon his return he is still
negotiating . . . "give me a job out on the back forty." What
is he saying? He is saying that he is still autonomous, demanding. He did not wish to return to "church"; he had no intention
of facing the "Elder Brother"; he would not live with the
community. "I will come home"; "I will work hard" . . . but
only away from human relationships! What is the difference
in verse 21 from verses 18,19? *VERSE 20!* "And he arose, and
came to his father. But when he was yet a great way off,

13

his father saw him, and had compassion, and ran, and fell on his neck, and kissed him." The difference is grace! Will God run? *YES!* The Prodigal, like most of us, merely wished a business transaction, "Father, you do this then I will do that." The surprise of grace! He did not receive what he deserved— he received what he needed! The father saw him . . . had compassion . . . and ran . . . and fell on his neck . . . and kissed him! *GRACE!* Marvelous grace! The Prodigal saw an older, broken-hearted Dad run! He saw grace! The Elder Brother never saw grace! The Elder Brother did not want grace! The Elder Brother rejected grace! But not the Prodigal! He gave up! He said, "Dad, I'm yours!" I will no longer negotiate. I will go before the "church"; I will face the "Elder Brother"; I will live in town! If you can love me like this I can do anything for you. This is the awesome demand of grace!

An Obedience Of Faith

"But by the grace of God I am what I am: and his grace which was bestowed upon me was not in vain; but I laboured more abundantly than they all: yet not I, but the grace of God which was with me" (1 Cor. 15:10). Paul titles obedience as the "obedience of faith" (Rom. 1:5; 16:26). It is not faith in our obedience. It is simply an obedience of faith.

A faith that does not work lacks credibility.
A hope that does not endure lacks reality.
A love that does not serve lacks integrity.

Man does not merely hear to hear. He hears the glorious Gospel. He hears about grace, Christ, the cross. Tell men what God did before you tell men what to do. Man does not believe in believing. Faith is total trust in what God in Christ did at Calvary. No longer is faith in what one believes or does. Faith is now in Christ—who He is and what He does. Faith is not in performance nor perfection. Faith is reliance in the blood. Man does not repent merely intellectually. He does not merely admit he is wrong, "a little here and there." Repentance is not self-perserration! But as man sees the cross better he sees his own sins and deepest needs. He sees sin as God sees it. He accepts God's answer. He has an entirely different mind-set. Man does not merely confess to confess. With all his heart he confesses Christ (Acts 8:37-40). He denies self to trust Jesus. Hope is now based upon the precious name of Jesus. Man is not merely baptized to join a church, obey a command. Baptism is man physically, viably, visibly, totally "putting Christ on" (Rom. 6:3,4; Col. 2:12; Gal. 3:24-29). Baptism without Christ and His cross is nothing. Baptism is passive. It is the only thing man does without doing anything! Man hears, believes, repents, confesses—but another man baptizes him. This is demonstrating man's faith in the cross and not with self. Man is baptized into the control of the Father, Son, and Holy Spirit. Baptism is not a meritorious work of man! Baptism is faith accepting Christ. Why do men serve as missionaries? suffer? give? work? Simply because of grace. The more grace one brings in the more obedience one puts out. "For ye are bought with a price: therefore glorify God in your body, and in your spirit, which are God's" (1 Cor. 6:20).

> To run and work the law commands
> Yet gives me neither feet nor hands.
> But better news the Gospel brings;
> It bids me fly, and gives me wings.

Questions

1. Begin each lesson magnifying God, Christ, grace!
2. Discuss MMLJ and Acts! Is this our mistake?
3. Discuss how Christ is the focus of all sermons in Acts.
4. Why do men reject, fight grace? Discuss.
5. Discuss Deism.
6. Does grace eliminate obedience? works? Discuss.
7. Discuss "intake" versus "output."
8. Discuss the cost of grace to God and us.
9. Discuss Luke 15:20—the key verse. Are you like the Prodigal? the Elder Son?

LESSON 3

Falling From Grace

Introduction

AMAZING GRACE! Tell men what God did before you tell men what to do! Focus upon grace; build everything upon the majesty of God. The glory of Christianity is God. Tell people about God, the Good God, the Father of our Lord and Savior Jesus Christ. Tell men there is hope at the cross of Christ. *GRACE—GRACE—GRACE!!* But what do we really know and preach about grace? Many simply know, believe, teach, yea emphasize, "one can fall from grace." This is all some wish to hear preached about grace. In many pulpits there have been more sermons on "Falling From Grace" than "Grace." How tragic! "Falling From Grace" is part of orthodoxy to some. A believer (Christian) can fall from grace. The fact of apostasy is valid. *ANY MAN, ANYWHERE, AT ANY TIME, CAN GO TO HELL!* "Falling From Grace" must be believed yea preached. But "Grace" must also be preached! *FIRST!* A preacher was fired. Perhaps for many reasons—who knows? But the reason given? "You are preaching grace . . . we wish sermons on "fire and brimstone." This was one shock in my young ministry—to be assailed because of grace. Preaching grace can keep one in "hot water." *INCREDIBLE!* Yet true! There are "professional misunderstanders" and "malicious misrepresenters." Have you ever heard of a preacher's being fired for preaching "works"? Grace demands works, but works has no place for grace. What thrills you about grace? That we have it? Or that "one can fall from grace"? We are saved by grace; don't you ever forget it.

17

Falling From Grace

"Christ is become of no effect unto you, whosoever of you are justified by the law; ye are fallen from grace. For we through the Spirit wait for the hope of righteousness by faith. For in Jesus Christ neither circumcision availeth anything, nor uncircumcision; but faith which worketh by love" (Gal. 5:4-6).

Calvinism is wrong; one can fall from grace. There are five major tenets of Calvinism; they are usually presented by the TULIP acrostic:

> T otal depravity
> U nconditional election
> L imited atonement
> I rresistible grace
> P erseverance

Calvinism is wrong in all five! As someone observed:

> If you seek it you cannot find it,
> If you find it you cannot get it,
> If you get it you cannot lose it,
> If you lose it you never had it!

"Once saved; always saved" is both unscriptural and non-sensible. Adam and Eve were lost . . . Israel was lost . . . at times David was lost . . . Judas . . . Demas. The entire book . of Hebrews warns against apostasy. One cannot be protected against himself in spite of himself. One can come . . . but one also can go (read John 6). Christianity is a life—not a monumental split second. We can be saved then stuck. "Once saved, always saved" is wrong! "Once saved, barely saved" is equally wrong! Eternal security is wrong—but eternal insecurity is equally wrong. The possibility of apostasy must not be preached as the probability of apostasy. Don't turn the "Good News" into "Bad News." Don't turn Christian joy into sorrow.

Familiar scriptures need to be read more closely! Read Gal. 5 again! Slowly. Notice what is said. Christians can fall from *GRACE!* We do not fall from law, works, even the church. We fall from *GRACE!* The Galatians fell—not because of heinous sins—but from turning aside from grace to law. This is the eternal thrust of legalism. It is easier to turn the whole system into a legalistic method one can control . . . a system through which one can buy his way back into God's approval with religious works. Today we do the same thing. We try to win, to control God's love and approval in a strange, religious barter system. We try *to* work to grace not *from* grace.

The answer to "falling" is, naturally, "standing." "By Silvanus, a faithful brother unto you, as I suppose, I have written briefly, exhorting, and testifying that this is the true grace of God wherein ye stand" (1 Pet. 5:12). "By whom also we have access by faith into this grace wherein ye stand, and rejoice in hope of the glory of God" (Rom. 5:2). ". . . yea, he shall be holden up: for God is able to make him stand" (Rom. 14:4). "Moreover, brethren, I declare unto you the gospel which I preached unto you, which also ye have received, and wherein ye stand" (1 Cor. 15:1). ". . . for by faith ye stand" (2 Cor. 1:24). It is true one can fall from grace. How does one know? The Bible says so! It is equally true one can stand in grace. How does one know? The Bible says so! Both positions must be believed and preached. If one can know he is fallen with certainty why cannot he equally know with certainty he is standing? One is saved by grace; one then continues to stand in grace. One is saved by grace; one is kept by grace. The process that saves a man continues to keep that man. The answer to divorce is marriage; the answer to instrumental music is singing; the answer to falling is standing.

> Not the labors of my hands
> Can fulfill Thy law's demands;
> Could my zeal no respite know,
> Could my tears forever flow,
> All for sin could not atone,
> Thou must save, and thou alone.

Blessed Assurance, Jesus Is Mine

God wants *ALL* His children to be assured! "And this is the record, that God hath given to us eternal life, and this life is in his Son. He that hath the Son hath life; and he that hath

19

not the Son of God hath not life. These things have I written unto you that believe on the name of the Son of God; that ye may know that ye have eternal life, and that ye may believe on the name of the Son of God" (1 Jn. 5:11-13). One may be wrong about many things but not grace. Claim grace! Trust Jesus! To have Christ is to have eternal life. Do you have Jesus? One cannot have Jesus and be lost.

Assurance is not arrogance. "Wherefore let him that thinketh he standeth take heed lest he fall" (1 Cor. 10:12). Familiar scriptures must be read more closely. One can fall; arrogance is lethal. But this verse does not teach one has already fallen! One is in jeopardy, but one had not fallen. The Church is not the Savior; Jesus is the Savior. The Church is the saved! Upon this all agree. "Then why doesn't the Church act like it?" We cannot assure others if we are not sure ourselves. Can one sing "Blessed Assurance" with enthusiasm? Is this song scriptural? If it is, can one also preach what one sings? Must there be contradictions in our singing and preaching? Do you sing "Blessed Assurance" with your fingers crossed?

"Wherefore, my beloved, as ye have always obeyed, not as in my presence only, but now much more in my absence, work out your own salvation with fear and trembling. For it is God which worketh in you both to will and to do of his good pleasure" (Phil. 2:12,13). This is another passage that has not been read closely. When you quote a verse do you know the verse in front of it and the one after it? If not, then you probably do not know the one you are quoting. This is "proof-texting" or "scripture lifting." This abuses the text. The word "work out" means "mine out" not human attainment. Grace gave a gold mine. "Thanks be to God for his unspeakable gift" (2 Cor. 9:15). God has provided. The gold mine is there. God is not stingy! The amount used is up to us. But also quote verse 13—"God works in us." Christianity is not self-reliance. The strength of Christianity is God not man.

Another example of familiar scriptures is Eph. 6:17, "And take the helmet of salvation, and the sword of the Spirit, which is the word of God." We promote the last of this verse to ignore the first. The helmet of salvation is assurance! One cannot be a "soul winner" bare-headed! Imagine a "soul winner" out door-knocking. He says to a sinner, "Are you saved?" The sinner answers "Are you?" He stutters, looks away, blabbers, then mutters, "I cannot know." How can we offer salvation to a sinner if we don't know if we have it ourselves? Again, it usually takes about ten minutes for a sinner baptized to dress. Brethren hug this new brother with joy. *WONDERFUL!* No one would doubt his conversion. But can the God who kept him saved ten minutes keep him saved ten years? Do we believe more in the baptistry than Christ? After baptism is it all down hill? Some wish they had died in the baptistry. Their theology should be "baptize them then shoot them." Absurd!

Assurance is in Christ. It is not perfection, performance. One can never know enough! Salvation is by grace. Yet our legalistic concepts defeat us. We have a "Las Vegas Slot Machine Mentality." We must be at the right place, at the right time, doing the right thing when Jesus returns. This is futile! This trusts performance, place, luck! To its ultimate this means one has to die at the right infinitesimal split-second to be saved. This means our faith is in "dying right"—not in Christ. Few will "hit" that split-second! Such legalism is ridiculous. One cannot sleep at night expecting his "legalistic roof" to fall in on him! Brethren have guilt but not grace. They respond in tears with the intention, "I will try harder." Bad matters become worse. Man cannot save himself by himself; he cannot keep himself by himself. As one preacher said, in a sermon, "Point #1, no sin shall enter heaven. Point #2, all sin and fall short of the glory of God." Beware of "Joy Robbers." It is a crime to steal joy from brethren! God cannot use a man that does not know he is converted! Any church without assurance will never do much. Beware of any pulpit that consistently makes you feel worse than when you came. As one member said of worship, "Let's go get our weekly beating." How tragic! Someone bragged upon a preacher's sermon, "You really stepped on my toes today!" The preacher sadly answered, "Either your feet were up high off the floor or my arm was mightly low . . . I was aiming at your heart." The idea that a faithful Christian's chances are "slim or none" negates the Gospel. All over brethren are living with doom and gloom. Some, pathetically, have decided "they cannot make it." The cardinal virtue of Christianity is not "grit"; it is joy! Joy is the fruit of grace. *BELIEVE IT! ENJOY IT!*

21

One other area demands attention. This involves inferiority. Some cannot accept grace because this would give them worth. They, therefore, conclude grace is for others not for them. They have the idea the blood of Jesus can handle this sin of others but not theirs. This is a blanket rejection of the love of God and the power of blood. This is actually a cop-out! God loves the world; Jesus died for all. Accept it!

Legalism Gone To Seed

Yet our old mentality dies hard. The "Weight and Balance" concept of salvation . . . God literally dropped a Bible out of the sky with a note saying, "Good Luck." This is Deism. This makes grace law. This reduces Christianity to a business transaction. Like a yo-yo Christians are saved and lost a million times daily. No wonder legalistic Christians crack up!

Another mentality connects salvation with our prayers. Prayer is not to be minimized, but this concept has one being lost in-between prayers. If Jesus returned and we were not praying then we are lost. Jesus probably will not find all of us at prayer. This gets us back to a place, time, and performance. Consistency demands perfection. One adherent allowed 2% error! One could be 2% off in knowledge or performance. Where is this 2% scripture? This is "legalism gone to seed." This is the total failure of self-reliance. It is claiming grace while practicing law. It is futile.

Grace does not encourage carelessness. Read Rom. 6:1,2. A child reared in a home of trust can develop into a healthy, matured adult! A child reared in uncertainty and distrust will develop into one social problem. Grace involves a relationship. It is of faith not perfection. I am married. I am not a perfect husband but I am faithful. We have a great home. There are no perfect parents but there are faithful parents. There are no perfect elders but there are faithful elders. God did not command us to be successful; He does demand faithfulness. Ours is a grace-faith system as opposed to a law-works system. We trust God; He also trusts us! God is not only preparing heaven for us; He is preparing us for heaven. Salvation is neither a fire-escape from judgment nor an insurance policy against hell.

22

God does not wish His children to live on the knife-edge of uncertainty! "To the praise of the glory of his grace, wherein he hath made us accepted in the beloved" (Eph. 1:6). "There is therefore now no condemnation to them which are in Christ Jesus, who walk not after the flesh, but after the Spirit. For the law of the Spirit of life in Christ Jesus hath made me free from the law of sin and death" (Rom. 8:1,2). Claim the finished work of Christ! Be faithful (literally one full of faith). It is a disgrace not to accept grace.

Cheese And Crackers

A young man had a foreign background. The goal of his life was to return to the "Old Country," Europe, the land of his ancestors. He saved and saved then bought a boat ticket. A cruise ship ticket buys gourmet meals. The young man did not know this. When the meal bells sounded he quietly went to his room alone to eat cheese and crackers. As the boat docked he excitedly shared his dream with a fellow-passenger. He then concluded, "The only bad thing was missing the meals and fellowship." The man exclaimed, "Didn't you know the meals came with the ticket?"

Beloved, assurance, certainty, joy come with the ticket!

Questions

1. Magnify God, Christ, grace.
2. Study in detail Gal. 5:4-6. Study what it says plus what it does not say.
3. What is the simple answer to falling from grace?
4. Can Christians sing "Blessed Assurance"? Because of grace or performance?
5. Are you legalistic? If not, why not?
6. Where is assurance?
7. What is the hallmark virtue of Christianity?
8. Are you saved? Right now? This minute?

LESSON 4

By Grace Through Faith

Introduction

AMAZING GRACE! Sing it! Preach it! Believe it! Praise
God for it! Tell men what God did before you tell men what
to do. "But we preach Christ crucified" (1 Cor. 1:23). What
a magnificent cause! A congregation with a new building
wanted a sign to state the Restoration Plea. They chose this
statement. Time passed. A vine grew and covered the last two
words, "Christ crucified." "But we preach" was left visible.
This story represents many congregations. They are sound,
active, generous. They have a huge "plant" seating hundreds.
But they are declining, yea dying. "Church Growth Experts"
are brought in. Excellent lectures, methods. But things continue to go from bad to worse. *WHY?* Because the preaching
is only preaching! "Christ crucified" is absent! Never have
we had better preachers, more sermons, and greater lessons.
The essence/power of Christianity is the cross. It is not
preaching, per se, but the content. 1 Cor. 1:21 literally means,
"the foolishness of the things preached." Gospel preaching
begins, continues, and ends with Christ. The focus is Christ;
the glory is Christ. The Gospel must not be reduced to abstract
religious law. The Gospel must never be narrowed to issues
and pet peeves. It is not enough to preach—we must preach
"Christ crucified." The vine covering the sign must be cut
down. The substance of the church must be restored. Churches
that focus upon the cross will become strong and grow.
Churches that neglect the cross will die. Deservedly so,
". . . which I have received of the Lord Jesus, to testify the
gospel of the grace of God" (Acts 20:24). "For I determined
not to know anything among you, save Jesus Christ, and him

crucified" (1 Cor. 2:2). "But God forbid that I should glory, save in the cross of our Lord Jesus Christ, by whom the world is crucified unto me, and I unto the world" (Gal. 5:14). Are we *REALLY* preaching the cross? Christ? Is this our distinctive plea? We are saved by grace—don't you ever forget it!

Only By Grace But Not Grace Only

Christianity is not works-law; it is grace-faith! ". . . by grace ye are saved . . . For by grace are ye saved through faith; and that not of yourselves: it is the gift of God: not of works, lest any man should boast. For we are his workmanship, created in Christ Jesus unto good works, which God hath before ordained that we should walk in them" (Eph. 2:5, 8-10). To undersand this is vital. Christianity is a grace-faith system. God provides and man accepts. God gives and man receives. Salvation, 100%, was totally produced by God. Man appropriates what God did. Salvation is not a business transaction. Salvation is wholly of God. Everything, ultimately, depends upon God's grace. Go there, live there, stay there. "And to be found in him, not having mine own righteousness, which is of the law, but that which is through the faith" (Phil. 3:9). The Apostle Paul stands as the most marvelous trophy of the grace of God this world has ever seen!

But grace had to act, do, live, work! Grace without works is dead! There was no Savior until there was a cross. "For he hath made him to be sin for us, who knew no sin; that we might be made the righteousness of God in him" (2 Cor. 5:21). "For the grace of God that bringeth salvation hath appeared unto all men, teaching us that, denying ungodliness and worldly lusts, we should live soberly, righteously, and godly, in this present world" (Tit. 2:11,12). "And the grace of our Lord was exceeding abundant with faith and love which is in Christ Jesus" (1 Tim. 1:14). "Who hath saved us, and called us with an holy calling, not according to our works, but according to his own purpose and grace, which was given us in Christ Jesus before the world began" (2 Tim. 1:9). Grace had to act to give.

26

My hope is built on nothing less
Than Jesus blood and righteousness
I dare not trust the sweetest frame,
But wholly lean on Jesus' name.

A sinner can earn death but he cannot earn life. Life is a gift!
Christianity is the only religion that makes human insufficiency
the gateway to blessing. "Let us keep our eyes fixed on Jesus,
on whom our faith depends from beginning to end" (Heb. 12:2
GNB). Grace teaches, touches, changes, strengthens.

Only By Faith But Not Faith Only

Salvation is a grace-faith system. Grace acted in Christ on
a cross. Faith, likewise, is active. John Calvin said, "While
it is faith alone that justifies, the faith that justifies is never
alone." If grace had not acted man could not be saved. If faith
does not act man still cannot be saved. Grace is not universalism! God will not coerce man into heaven. God justified—
but man of his own will must accept. Martin Luther said, "The
evidence of our faith is our acceptance of grace." Two liberties
are involved: (1) The sovereign liberty of God the subject, and
(2) the liberty of man he solicits. Grace does not violate either.
To justify is a Divine perogative; human faith is a confession
of allegiance. Grace says, "You belong to me"; faith says,
"I belong to you." Grace is God's action against sin; faith
is the acceptance of that Gospel. Man's pride stands against
faith. Some, in human pride, feel too unworthy to accept
unearned, unmerited, and undeserved salvation. Soren
Kierkegaard said, "Whoever perceives that he cannot do even
the least thing without God . . . is nearer to perfection. And
whoever understands himself thus and finds nothing at all pain-
ful in the awareness—whose mind feels no shame in letting
other people see that he can do nothing himself . . . but in
whose heart joy always conquers because he jubilantly . . .
throws himself into the arms of God . . . who can do all things.
Aye, such a man is indeed the perfect man." It is never God
who denies grace but the malice and pride of human will which
refuses to accept it. Some can never be saved—only because
they will not let God save them.

Faith is but the bumbling hand that receives the grace of God. Man is saved by faith and kept by faith. Jesus dwells in our hearts by faith. God ventured all to save us in Christ; faith ventures all to accept Him. Remember! We cannot do what God alone did! Also, God will not do what we alone must do. You cannot do anything to pay for your salvation. Faith does not pay for salvation. There is no human merit in faith. Man is justified *BY* faith not *FOR* faith. Faith does not earn anything; it enables God to do His thing. Faith by its very nature must be tried. A faith that cannot be tried cannot be trusted. Job said, "Tho he slay me, yet will I trust him" (Job 13:15). Faith is the heroic effort of life—wherein one flings himself in reckless trust on God.

Therefore faith is the principle of life: ". . . but the just shall live by faith." This is quoted three times in the New Testament with three different applications. The only obvious response to grace is faith. That faith is not without obedience. One who believes is obedient, and only he who is obedient believes. "Faith without works is dead" (James 2). If the medicine remains in the bottle on the shelf it cannot cure. The grace of God is accepted by faith. Obedience is the response of faith to the grace of God. In order to receive it man must believe it; in order to enjoy it man must obey it. Faith does not destroy good works—only the claim to justification by good works. Faith totally casts itself upon the grace of God.

Faith In Christ Not Faith In Faith

Moderns have a great problem with "believing." They, basically, believe in believing. Faith is magic, superstition, sentimentality. Observe these daily statements, "I wish I had more faith." "I wish I had your faith," "If only I had more faith." The modern conclusion is "believe and all is well." Faith is reduced to human works, the ultimate positive thinking. Bluntly, faith is reduced to will power.

But faith has no power in itself. Faith is in its object. Faith can be no stronger than its object. To illustrate. A huge bulldozer is stuck hopelessly in mud. Another bulldozer comes to pull it out. Would a string do? a rope? a small chain? Of course not! Faith cannot make a string stronger or a powerful chain weaker! To pull the bulldozer out you would need a powerful chain. Faith using that chain could free the bulldozer. But there would be no glory in the man believing. Beware of any man proud of his faith. The power is in the object. The chain gets the glory. Man in sin is hopelessly stuck. Jesus is the only chain that can free. My believing or disbelieving does not alter His power. When utilized the glory is His. There is no glory to the believer—only the object! It is not faith in God but faith in a great God! It is Christ power not will power. Faith is never dangerous until one acts upon it. Only the *doer* of the word is the real *hearer* (James 1:25-27). Faith grows in us as we obey. God alone can save; God alone can keep. The same faith that got you saved will keep you saved. We are kept by the power of God through faith. Faith gives God the glory because Jesus Christ is the Savior. Had you rather have little faith in a strong plank or a strong faith in a weak plant? *YOU CANNOT UNDERSTAND FAITH UNTIL YOU UNDERSTAND GRACE!* To know grace is to develop faith. Faith does not know where it is being led—but faith does know who is leading. Faith that is sure of itself is not faith; faith that is sure of God is faith. The "core issue" . . . man's relationship with God. Christianity is vitally concerned in *what* a man trusts. It is not a question of whether or not there is faith but faith in what? Do we trust what we do or who Christ is? God will never do anything *TO* nor *WITH* nor *FOR* us without our faith. God uses us; God uses our lives.

To Believe Is To Belong

Man is an activist. He uses his works to explain away faith. He uses his deeds to explain away grace. Man thinks that belonging will result in believing. This is not so. The reverse is true. Man thinks activity will produce faith; this may not be so. The reverse is true! *TO BELIEVE IS TO BELONG!* Belief in old English is "bylief." How you live is actually what you believe. Let's be honest with ourselves. You cannot divorce faith from life.

Moment by moment, I'm kept in His love;
Moment by moment, I've life from above:
Looking to Jesus, the glory doth shine;
Moment by moment, Oh Lord, I am thine.

Much is said today about commitment. Christianity, obviously, is commitment—it is a total commitment. But two things precede commitment. Commitment proves futile without these two things.

(1) Radical surrender. Christianity is a grace-faith not works-law system. God did not drop the Bible out of the sky saying, "Good luck." Works-law is human effort. Man is the master of his fate and the captain of his soul. Works-law is performance oriented. "More-more-more." It is will power. "Try harder." Works-law is perfection. James said to fail in one part was to bear the wrath to all. Consequently grace-faith is a total rejection of self. Grace-faith is not right answers to selected questions. Grace-faith is not the ability to pass a religious quiz at the judgment. Having to be right "on all the issues" is shaky ground. *FACE IT!* No legal system can save sinners. Grace . . . the cross of Christ . . . terminated/eliminated the law principle (Col. 2:14-17). Christianity is not another "spruced-up," "warmed-over" Law of Moses! Law cannot grasp a redeemer! Law has no place for a redeemer! Only by the law is the knowledge of sin. You cannot come to Calvary by way of Sinai! Man surrenders his self-reliance, his self-sufficiency. Man dies to self. Grace is the key feature of God's relation to the world. God reaches down into the core of the meaning and need of man's life. Man never outgrows—gets beyond his need for God. Before commitment there must be radical surrender.

(2) Total trust. Couples commit themselves to marriage. Then fail. Why? Because they did not make that previous radical surrender. Many moderns make "decisions for Jesus" that quickly fail. They did not make that prior surrender. "If you artificially get them you will have to artificially keep them." Before commitment there must be a total trust! One now surrendered from self can cast himself upon the finished work of the cross. Our trust is totally in Jesus—who He is and what He did! What a relief! To trust Him by faith and not

our performance! Believing rather than achieving! Faith not perfection. But human effort dies hard. "Heaven helps those who help themselves." "I don't know if I can hold out." "If anyone makes it, he will." This brings us back again to law-works. When the cross is neglected one returns to legalism. Legalism is making salvation dependent upon law and one's ability to keep it. Legalism is trusting one's own performance for salvation. Legalism fails. Grace frees us from law-works! Grace frees us to love God and obey Him. Law-works is external. The principle is working within from without. Grace-faith is internal. The life of Jesus in us. This is the principle of working from within to without. Christ has freed us from the curse of the law. Trust Him!

Now man is ready to commit! Man's faith loving trusts the grace of God. ". . . but faith which worketh by love" (Gal. 5:6). God receives all the glory because salvation is by grace (Rom. 3:21-31; 4:3-5; 4:16-21; 11:6). Paul said all he was was by the grace of God (1 Cor. 15:10). Moralism is always the ever-present threat to the Gospel. For it short-circuits the Gospel by approaching the Bible—not to find out how it reveals the Gospel—but to derive applications from it for life, the Bible then becomes a compendium of moral teaching and makes Jesus only a philosophic, moral teacher. Believing the Gospel becomes "following the teachings of Jesus" rather than entrusting our lives totally to Him. Christianity is Christ! "I am the way, the truth, and the life: no man cometh unto the Father, but by me" (Jn. 14:6). "Neither is there salvation in any other: for there is none other name under heaven given among men, whereby we must be saved" (Acts 4:12). "But of him are ye in Christ Jesus, who of God is made unto us wisdom, and righteousness, and sanctification, and redemption: that, according as it is written, He that glorieth, let him glory in the Lord" (1 Cor. 1:20,31).

Salvation is simply by grace through faith!

Questions

1. Discuss the "Church Sign" where there is much preaching but no cross.
2. Could grace save by grace only or did grace have to act? Discuss the same reality with faith. Discuss the futility of self reliance.
3. Discuss only by faith but not faith only.
4. Do we believe in believing? Can this faith save?
5. Discuss "To believe is to belong."
6. Discuss surrender, trust, then commitment.

LESSON 5

Power Of Grace

Introduction

AMAZING GRACE! Tell men what God did before you tell men what to do. The only permanent motivation in Christianity is grace. What *draws* sinners *keeps* Christians. "And as Moses lifted up the serpent in the wilderness, even so must the Son of Man be lifted up" (Jn. 3:14). "And I, if I be lifted up from the earth, will draw all men unto me. This he said, signifying what death he should die" (Jn. 12:32,33). "But unto them which are called, both Jews and Greeks, Christ the power of God, and the wisdom of God" (1 Cor. 1:24).

> How I love the great Redeemer
> Who is doing so much for me;
> With what joy I tell the story
> Of the love that makes men free.

Christianity must not be reduced to "Positive Religious Thinking." It is not the "Ultimate PMA Rally." Christianity is also more than a code of ethics, a standard of religious performance. Christianity is Christ. You can take Buddha out of Buddhism and still have Buddhism. When you take Christ out of Christianity there is nothing left. Christianity is a personal relationship with Jesus. Christianity is not personal *trying;* it is total *trusting!* Our faith is in Him. It is not struggling; it is abiding. "Abide in me and I in you. As the branch cannot bear fruit of itself, except it abide in the vine; no more can ye, except in me . . . for without me ye can do nothing" (Jn. 15:4,5). Human merit, power is completely ruled out in the victorious Christian life.

33

And every virtue we possess
And every victory won
And every thought and holiness
Are His alone.

When we depend upon man, we get only what man can do; when we depend on grace, we get what God can do. No wonder so many Christians are weak and frustrated—they are trying to do God's work under human power. It will not work. God *BOTH* saves and enables! "Whereby are given unto us exceeding great and precious promises: that by these ye might be partakers of the divine nature, having escaped the corruption that is in the world through lust" (2 Pet. 1:4). We are saved by grace; don't you ever forget it!

To Be/Do What They Were/Did — We Must Have The Power They Had

Restoration is to be what they were and do what they did and teach what they taught. But there is more—to be and do what they were requires the power they had. This is usually never considered. The key to restoration is to utilize their power, "But ye shall receive power, after that the Holy Ghost is come upon you: and ye shall be witnesses unto me both in Jerusalem, and in all Judea, and in Samaria, and unto the uttermost part of the earth" (Acts 1:8). Apostles could not be witnesses until they had the power! Tragically, power is usually incorrectly defined! Power is more than the miraculous, that which involves revelation. The apostles did work miracles, they did reveal truth. However power involved life . . . who they were and what they did. The power enabled the work. You cannot succeed in the work without the power. Christianity is *intake* not *output!* It is not self-reliance in human effort. Intake determines output. The power within causes the life without. "And hope maketh not ashamed: because the love of God is shed abroad in our hearts by the Holy Ghost which is given unto us" (Rom. 5:5). Christianity emphasizes what God does rather than what we do. "And with great power gave the apostles witness of the resurrection of the Lord Jesus: and great grace was upon them all" (Acts 4:33). "As ye have therefore received Christ Jesus the Lord, so walk ye in him" (Col. 2:6). Being confident of this very thing, that he which both begun a good work in you will perform it until the day of Jesus Christ" (Phil. 1:6). "Finally, my brethren, be strong in the Lord, and in the power of his might" (Eph. 6:10). We are to be strong "in the Lord," not in self. Christianity is not the power of self-determination. "But my God shall supply all your need according to his riches in glory by Christ Jesus" (Phil. 4:19). "Not that we are sufficient of ourselves to think anything as of ourselves; but our sufficiency is of God" (2 Cor. 3:5).

One of the greatest illustrations of grace-power involves the Macedonians. Read 2 Cor. 8,9. The poor Macedonian gave beyond "his power." The Bible says this motivation was grace. Giving is classified as a grace. It was by "grace" that Jesus (rich) became poor. From beginning to end the issue is grace. "And God is able to make all grace abound toward you; that ye, always having all sufficiency in all things, may abound to every good work" (2 Cor. 9:8). God is able to make us able. God saves; God enables. One is saved by grace; one must be kept by grace. "And by their prayer for you, which long after you for the exceeding grace of God in you. Thanks be unto God for his unspeakable gift" (2 Cor. 9:14,15).

Paul's Motivation Was Grace

All admire, eulogize Paul! He is the preacher's preacher, the Christians model. When you think of Christianity you think of Paul; when you think of Paul you think of Christianity. Paul changed radically; Paul preached; Paul was a missionary, debater, writer. Few men can claim to be/do what Paul was/did! *PAUL!* Yet, therein is a misunderstanding. Most make Paul a giant 10′ tall! "Superman" with a cape! A man who could out-think, outwork, and outlive any. But is this the true Paul? Read 2 Cor. 11. Paul did recite his performance. No man can equal his. Yet he did this reluctantly . . . embarrassed! This was not the power of Paul. *WHAT?* Paul's power was not Paul! His name, tribe, family, Phariseeism, ability were all rejected! "But what things were gain to me, those I counted loss for Christ. Yea doubtless, and I count all things but loss for the excellency of the knowledge of Christ Jesus my Lord: for whom I have suffered the loss of all things, and do count them but dung, that I may win Christ, and be found in him, not having mine own righteousness, which is of the law, but that which is through the faith of Christ, the righteousness which is of God by faith: That I may know him, and the power of his resurrection, and the fellowship of his sufferings, being made conformable unto his death" (Phil. 3:7-10). What a declaration! Paul was not a great missionary because he was a great man; he was a great missionary because he had a great God.

Although Paul had a great mind and discipline he was not physically impressive. Tradition says he was little, bald, crooked in his legs, and hooked-nosed. Perhaps we would be deeply shocked—yea disappointed—with Paul if we could see him. Honestly, could he get a "preaching-job" among us? A bachelor? ugly? some bad references? "For his letters, say they, are weighty and powerful; but his bodily presence is weak, and his speech contemptible" (2 Cor. 10:10).

Paul's power was grace! His glory was given to God! The most marvelous trophy of the grace of God this world has ever seen! With Paul it was *intake* not *output*. "The love of Christ motivated us" (2 Cor. 5:14). "But by the grace of God I am what I am: and his grace which was bestowed upon me was not in vain; but I labored more abundantly than they all: yet not I, but the grace of God which was with me" (1 Cor. 15:10). Grace-power! The power of Paul was grace. Grace enables one to be what God wants him to be, to do what God wants him to do. "Do your best and God will do the rest" is blasphemy. Our best works are but "filthy rags." Of himself man can do nothing. From the smallest to the greatest everything is grace. "I can do all things through Christ which strengtheneth me" (Phil. 4:13). "For to me to live is Christ, and to die is gain" (Phil. 1:21). "Let this mind be in you, which was also in Christ Jesus" (Phil. 2:5). "For I determined not to know anything among you, save Jesus Christ, and him crucified. And I was with you in weakness, and in fear, and in much trembling. And my speech and my preaching was not with enticing words of man's wisdom, but in demonstration of the Spirit and of power: that your faith should not stand in the wisdom of men, but in the power of God" (1 Cor. 2:2-5). "But God forbid that I should glory, save in the cross of our Lord Jesus Christ, by whom the world is crucified unto me, and I unto the world" (Gal. 6:14). No wonder so many of us are weak! We are trying to do God's will under human power. Paul knew the failure of law-works; he also knew the glory of grace-faith.

The greatest statement of grace versus self is found in 2 Cor. 12, "And lest I should be exalted above measure through the abundance of the revelations, there was given to me a thorn in the flesh, the messenger of Satan to buffet me, lest I should be exalted above measure. For this thing I besought the Lord thrice, that it might depart from me. And he said unto me, my grace is sufficient for thee: for my strength is made perfect in weakness. Most gladly therefore will I rather glory in my infirmities, that the power of Christ may rest upon me. Therefore I take pleasure in infirmities, in reproaches, in necessities, in persecutions, in distresses for Christ's sake: for when I am weak, then am I strong" (2 Cor. 12:7-10). Paul was even given a thorn to emphasize his power was grace! *AMAZING GRACE!*

Paul's Ministry Was Grace

Read Acts 20. Paul remembers his longest tenure lived at Ephesus. Paul knew his power was in God's mercy not Paul's merit. "Therefore seeing we have this ministry, as we have received mercy, we faint not" (2 Cor. 4:1). Since God would not give up on Paul, then Paul would never quit on God. Paul's ministry was of God, by God, and with God! Paul was not an "asset" to the church! He never thought he was doing God a favor by serving Him! Paul was humbled at the cross!

Paul's pulpit centered upon grace. "But none of these things move me, neither count I my life dear unto myself, so that I might finish my course with joy, and the ministry, which I have received, the Lord Jesus, to testify the gospel of the grace of God" (Acts 20:24). The church in Ephesus never lost their soundness (Rev. 2). However they misplaced grace . . . the Gospel . . . what God did! Too many pulpits merely preach—

but not the Gospel of grace. "And now, brethren, I commend you to God, and to the word of his grace, which is able to build you up, and to give you an inheritance among all them which are sanctified" (Acts 20:32). Churches can only be built on grace! Christians mature on grace. Paul was a grace-bought and grace-built man! Paul was not content to merely cope—in Christ he conquered. Christ is the author and finisher of our faith.

Paul's Ministry In Thessalonica

Perhaps the "Trophy of Grace" for congregations is Thessalonica. Scholars disagree on the exact time—length of ministry but it could not be more than a few months. Some say only a few weeks. But the young church survived yea grew! Paul wrote his two epistles within months of each other. One must read 1 Thess. 2 to determine Paul's strategy. Two major points are obvious:

(1) Paul told them what God had done. Paul preached unto them the Gospel of God. "But even after that we had suffered before, and were shamefully treated, as ye know, at Philippi, we were bold in our God to speak unto you the gospel of God with much contention" (1 Thess. 2:2). This congregation was not built upon "right answers to selected questions." This congregation did not grow because "it was right on all the issues." This congregation grew by conversions—not by proselyting! Their motivation was the grace of God—what God had done. It is not our love for God but His for us (1 Jn. 4:7-11). A grace-man is gracious. He carries/shares this grace with others. Paul, the man of grace, shared grace. "For all things are for your sakes, that the abundant grace might through the thanksgiving of many redound to the glory of God" (2 Cor. 4:15). Congregations bring in high-powered speakers to motivate. The result is temporary. The only permanent motivation is the grace of God. The more one grasps God's grace the more energetic he will be.

(2) Paul then told them what God had done to Paul. Many shy away farom "testifying." It can become infantile. But if God has not changed you then how could He change me? If

God has not helped you then how can be help me? If our lives remained unchanged and impotent—what, really, do we have to preach?

Read Acts 22,26. Paul relates his conversion. Why? To tell others that God saved/changed him so they could be saved/changed. Paul was a "satisfied customer." Paul was a model. If the grace of God could save Paul then it could save anyone. Paul was a living demonstration of the grace of God. Paul said, "Look at me." Paul always was totally shocked at the power of the Gospel that could save him. "Who was before a blasphemer, and a persecutor, and injurious: but I obtained mercy, because I did it ignorantly in unbelief. And the grace of our Lord was exceedingly abundant with faith and love which is in Christ Jesus. This is a faithful saying, and worthy of all acceptation, that Christ Jesus came into the world to save sinners; of whom I am chief. Howbeit for this cause I obtained mercy, that in me first Jesus Christ might shew forth all longsuffering, for a pattern to them which should hereafter believe on him to life everlasting" (1 Tim. 1:13-16). Paul never outgrew grace; he never "got over" grace.

Yet Paul did not glory in the personal aspect of this conversion. The Saturday Religious page did not commercialize, "Hear Paul tell of his conversion the 999th time!" Some sinners personally enjoy re-telling their sin and conversion. They glory in the telling. Paul was humbled! He was not proud of his sin-life. He did not embellish the blinding light and thundering voice aspects. He merely told others he first did what he wanted others to do. This is evangelism. Giving the Jesus we received to others.

This determined Paul's concept of ministry. He reminded them how he was gentle as a nurse with babies. "Mean preachers" have not received grace. They may preach grace as an intellectual fact but not as a received experience. One does not work to deserve grace. Because of grace one works. "For we are his workmanship, created in Christ Jesus unto good works, which God hath before ordained that we should walk in them" (Eph. 2:10). Paul further reminded the Thessalonicans how the "missionary team" had behaved. Grace changes character; character determines conduct. He then referred to his ministry as a loving father rearing his children,

"As ye know how we exhorted and comforted and charged everyone of you, as a father doth his children" (1 Thess. 2:11).

The power of Grace! We are saved by grace; don't you ever forget it.

Questions

1. Is Christianity PMA at its highest?
2. Have we neglected to find the power of the early Church as we strive to restore today?
3. Discuss how the apostles could not be missionaries without power.
4. Discuss Paul's motivation by grace. Are we trying to "out-do" Paul with our own human power?
5. Discuss *intake* versus *output*.
6. Discuss Paul's "thorn in the flesh."
7. From 1 Thess. 2 discuss Paul's concept of Church Growth.

LESSON 6

Grace In The Old Testament

Introduction

AMAZING GRACE! Shout it! Share it! Rejoice in it! Die with it! Tell men what God did before you tell men what to do. Truth is truth; the Gospel is truth; but the Gospel is more than truth. To illustrate. It is truth that cancer is bad. One cannot exaggerate the pain of cancer. One could preach this fact all over the world. This is truth but not Gospel. What, then, is Gospel? That there is a cure to cancer! This is the "Good News" of hope. It is truth that man is lost in sin. This must be preached. But to preach the damnation of sin without the cross solution is not Gospel. Preaching can become negative, futile, and self-defeating. The Gospel is grace, the cure is Christ, the cross. The Gospel is ". . . Jesus died for our sins" (1 Cor. 15:1-4). The Gospel is that sin can be forgiven and sinners reconciled. God justifies the ungodly. It is not, "What is the world coming to?" but "Who came into the world?" There is no sinner too evil for Christ to save; there is no Christian He cannot make better. Every sermon, lesson, method, project must come from the soil of hope. "The Lord is not slack concerning his promise, as some men count slackness; but is longsuffering to us-ward, not willing that any should perish, but that all should come to repentance" (2 Pet. 3:9). Jesus said, "Go ye into all the world, and preach the gospel to every creature" (Mk. 16:15). This is our privilege and task. We are not here to judge, to "straighten people out," merely to condemn. Sinners are to be convicted of their sins, but they are also to be given a Savior! Herald the Savior! Offer men hope in Christ! Preach the blood of the cross. Offer starving beggars bread! "And he is the propitation for our sins:

41

and not for ours only, but also for the sins of the whole world"
(1 Jn. 2:2). God is far more willing to save than we
preach/allow Him to be. Preach the grace of God. We are
saved by grace—don't you ever forget it!

The Old Testament Is Scripture, Too

This lesson is crucial. It will correct many misunderstandings
that have resulted in religious havoc. The Old Testament is
Bible, too! Bible students must understand the intimate relationship with the Old and New Testaments. Many neglect the
Old Testament. Some even justify this by saying their limited
time for study confines them to the New Testament. We even
carry a New Testament without the old. All Biblical originals
were written alone and often traveled alone. Why haven't these
so highly critical of translations awakened to the mistake of
Testaments? The Bible of Jesus was the Old Testament! The
written Bible of the early Church to a great degree was the
Old Testament. Early Gospel sermons (read Acts) were filled
with quotations from the Old Testament. The Law of Moses
was nailed to the cross but not the Old Testament! The Old
Testament revealed God; the New Testament reveals God. One
cannot know advanced math without first learning the math
tables. One cannot grasp the new until he knows the old! "All
scripture is given by inspiration of God, and is profitable for
doctrine, for reproof, for correction, for instruction in
righteousness: that the man of God may be perfect, thoroughly
furnished unto all good works" (2 Tim. 3:16,17). Now all these
things happen unto them for ensamples: and they are written
for our admonition, upon whom the ends of the world are
come" (1 Cor. 10:11). "For whatsoever things were written
aforetime were written for our learning, that we through
patience and comfort of the scriptures might have hope" (Rom.
15:4). "Wherefore the law was our schoolmaster to bring us
unto Christ, that we might be justified by faith" (Gal. 3:24).
"For Christ is the end of the law for righteousness to everyone
that believeth" (Rom. 10:4).

The Bible is a 66-book Bible! It must be studied as a total
unit. The Old Testament is not bad; it is not error. There is

no antagonism between the testaments. "Think not that I am come to destroy the law, or the prophets; I am not come to destroy, but to fulfill. For verily I say unto you, til heaven and earth pass, one jot or one tittle shall in no wise pass from the law, till all be fulfilled. Whosoever therefore shall break one of these least commandments, and shall teach men so, he shall be called least in the kingdom of heaven: but whosoever shall do and teach them, the same shall be called great in the kingdom of heaven" (Mt. 5:17-19). Jesus was born, lived, and died under Old Testament law. Do not neglect nor misunderstand the Old Testament.

God Is The Same In Both Testaments

This is the heart of much misunderstanding. Many believe God is evil in the Old and good in the New. *SACRILEGE!* "Jesus Christ the same yesterday, and today, and forever" (Heb. 13:5). "Every good gift and every perfect gift is from above, and cometh down from the Father of lights, with whom is no variableness, neither shadow of turning" (James 1:17). "I am Alpha and Omega, the first and the last" (Rev. 1:11). God is not a fickle pagan idol! God cannot be God and be subject to change! God is the same God in both Testaments! This is basic! All scriptural studies must come from this basic reality. God was not "converted" between the Testaments!

God has saved people by grace from the beginning. God has not changed . . . man has developed. My children are all now adult. I have not changed; but they progressed. When young they were controlled by rules and regulations. They now live under conscience. The God of grace revealed himself in primitive times by law. Paul says we are now under grace (Rom. 6:14). The same God revealing himself as people could bear it. God's grace provides and man's response is faith. This is universal and eternal. God did not begin with "law-keeping" then change suddenly into grace. Grace saved people under the law (Hebrews). The law could never save; it did produce a knowledge of sin (Rom. 3:20; 7:7-12). Only the Gospel (cross of Christ) can save.

We must keep the character of God "clean." God is not

a "mean guy in heaven" who delights in punishment. God wants to heal, restore, save! Wrath does not produce grace; grace demands wrath. The prophets were sent out saying for God, "All I wish to do is to love you." God wants to be our friend, our Lord, and our strength. The nature and character of God are not subject to change.

There Is Grace In The Old Testament

Our first two wrong assumptions have caused this fallacious conclusion. Most think that grace is not found in the Old Testament. But life itself is grace. Man did not invent himself. Man, of himself, deserves nothing. *Charis* (Greek) in the New Testament is basically the same as *chen* (Hebrew) in the Old Testament. "But the God of all grace, who hath called us unto his eternal glory by Christ Jesus, after that ye have suffered while, make you perfect, stablish, strengthen, settle you" (1 Pet. 5:10).

Immediately in Genesis God's grace spared the world. "But Noah found grace in the eyes of the Lord" (Gen. 6:8). Man, the world, deserved destruction. God saves the ancient world by grace.

Abraham best illustrates grace. Abraham was an idolator in a heathen world. He was not blessed because he deserved it; he was saved by God's election grace. Man chokes on "election grace." The Potter does have power over the clay. God will have mercy upon whom He will have mercy (Rom. 9:15). Well the scholar said, "How odd of God to choose the Jews!" They were not bigger, better, richer! Read Genesis 12-25. Then read Romans 4. Abraham is the father of the faithful. Yet Abraham's power was grace not self. All Abraham could make himself was an Ishmael. Abraham reveals the folly of human effort. He was called before the Law, before circumcision. Both Abraham and Sarah were impotent (Rom. 4:18-25). Israel is a "Son of Grace." It is hard for proud man to swallow election but God chose and blessed Israel because He wished to (Deut. 4:7,8,33,34; 6:10-12; 7:6-10; 9:4-7).

Throughout the history of Israel God was revealing His grace. "Stand still and see the salvation of the Lord." "I bore you on eagle's wings." God gave Israel Canaan! The sole of their bare feet guaranteed possession! To remove shoes indicates "Holy Ground." It was not their sandals but bare feet! They never possessed their possessions! They never claimed what God had already given them. Jericho fell by God's power not human merit. The Judges were illustration after illustration how Israel's power was God. God took obscure men with questionable backgrounds then used powerless methods (of man's thinking) to win battles. In the period of the Judges God was trying to show men the simplicity of the grace life.

Jonah is a book of grace. The Jew had forgotten his role in saving the world God's grace had been turned inward. The Jew would not share God nor His grace. In fact Jonah was totally aghast with the grace of God. He would not let God be God! The Jew, having grace, never appreciated it.

Hosea is the epitome of grace in the Old Testament. Through the catastrophic life of this prophet God revealed His love, mercy, and grace. God, in the Old Testament, was a God who stands, stoops, and stays! God was a promise-making and promise-keeping God. Habakkuk cried, ". . . but the just shall live by his faith" (Hab. 2:4). This is quoted three times (all different circumstances) in the New Testament (Rom. 1:17; Gal. 3:11; Heb. 10:38). There was grace in the Old Testament; there was faith in the Old Testament. Faith is trust, commitment. Faith in the Old Testament meant "to put one's weight down on." Faith meant one could commit all. Faith was a response to His faithfulness. It is a total response from the whole self. Faith is human response to the trustworthy character of God. Christianity is historical. It is not fantasy like idolatry; it is a total response from the whole self. Faith is human response to the trustworthy character of God. Christianity is historical. It is not fantasy like idolatry; it is not merely philosophy. Our faith is worthy because it is factual, historical, and human. The God of heaven came and acted upon the stage of human history. This is the glory of the grace of God.

Grace separates Christianity from the religions of man. Religion of man is a system of human works. Christianity is a revelation of divine grace. Forgiveness of sin from God to man is unique! Philosophy cannot even consider it. The Israelites were saved by grace. The Law, providence, and

Canaan were all gifts of grace. They had not earned, deserved, nor attained it. *GRACE!* Yet the Israelites stumbled over grace. Man has always been prone *to do* not simply *accept*. "All the Lord speaks we will do" (Ex. 19:8). Israel bargained with God. Salvation literally was reduced to a business transaction. It was easier for Israel to choose *law* than *grace*. It still is! Yet man cannot save himself by doing alone. Man chafes at ignorance, weakness, failure. Man rebels against spiritual bankruptcy. God gave Israel the Law to emphasize the need and glory of grace. The Jews became idolatrous with their law. It became National Patriotic Pride. The Law became "god." The Jew decided "to go it, alone." Well did Burton Coffman say, "Nothing that a man could do in a million years of righteous living could ever earn the tiniest fraction of the salvation God gives to men in Christ." "But we preach Christ crucified, unto the Jews a stumbling block" (1 Cor. 1:24). Jesus both in Isaiah and in the epistles is constantly called "the stone of stumbling." The Jews stumbled over grace. Yet do not be too harsh on them! The last thing man relinquishes is autonomy, self-control! Man wants to "call the shots," do his own thing. Peter rebuked Jesus for the very thought of death (Mt. 16). Jesus, in turn, rebuked Peter, "This, Peter, is what we all must do." We must die to live, fail to succeed, be last to be first, give to get, the way up is down. This is salvation/life by grace. Yet consciously or unconsciously we keep trying to balance our religious books. The Jew could not keep the Law. A man who cannot keep the Law must be saved by grace.

The Old Testament Was Totally External

Another false conclusion is that one could be perfect keeping the Law regardless of the condition of his heart. Actually, on the surface, this could not be! There is the letter of the law and the spirit of the law (2 Cor. 3). It is an injustice to reduce Judaism to external law-keeping. License ignores the nature of God; legalism ignores the nature of man. Grace revealed the law; tragically the Jew reduced the law to legalism. Chapter after chapter then was written by scribes on technicalities. The law became absurd.

This is so unnecessary. The tenth command was a heart command, "Thou shalt not covet" (Ex. 20; Deut. 5). God's laws were never intended to become technical regulations. The first two commands involve far more than externals. The Jews delighted in the fourth, "Remember the Sabbath Day." They had volumes on what man could or could not do. It became "silliness gone to seed." Legalism is not only law-keeping; it is law-depending. The Jews were not trying *to be* right they were content *to do* right.

Jesus was glad to answer the question, "What is the greatest command?" "Thou shalt love the Lord thy God with all thy heart, and with all thy soul, and with all thy mind. This is the first and great commandment. And the second is like unto it, Thou shalt love thy neighbor as thyself. On these two commandments hang all the law and the prophets" (Mt. 22:36-40). *WHAT!* Jesus answered a lawyer's question by quoting two Old Testament scriptures (Deut. 6:5; Levit. 19:18). Notice what Jesus did! He "ran" two scriptures together. He did not quote all the passage. He then concluded, "Upon these two commands hang all the law!" Love of God and love of neighbor. The Old Testament focused upon the heart! It was not enough to keep commands outwardly.

Jesus turned upon the Pharisees with a vengeance in Mt. 23. It was not their external rules! The outside was clean but the inside was not. "Woe unto you, scribes and Pharisees, hypocrites! For ye pay tithe of mint and anise and cummin, and have omitted the weightier matters of the law, judgment, mercy, and faith: these ought ye to have done, and not to leave the other undone" (Mt. 23:23). Jesus knew Micah, "He hath shewed thee, O man, what is good; and what doth the Lord require of thee, but to do justly, and to love mercy, and to walk humbly with thy God?" (Micah 6:8).

David considered this in Psalm 100. He first declares that "God is" (verse 3). Then he declared, "God is good" (verse 5). It is not enough to prove the existence of God. Sinners will not fall in love with arguments—even valid. Sinners must know that "God is good." Our children must be taught this. *GRACE!* Our God is a good God. Grace is primary—even in the Old Testament. We are saved by grace; don't you ever forget it.

Moment by moment, I'm kept in His love;
Moment by moment, I've life from above:
Looking to Jesus, the glory doth shine;
Moment by moment, Oh Lord, I am Thine!

Questions

1. Discuss the distinction between gospel and truth.
2. Do we read, study, treasure the Old Testament? Is it given its proper place?
3. Has God always been the same? Is there grace in the Old Testament? Discuss. Why has man always stumbled over grace?
4. Was the Old Testament completely external? Could one keep the law with an evil heart?
5. Discuss Mt. 22:36-40. Discuss the love of God, for self, and for neighbors.

The Gift Of Grace

Introduction

AMAZING GRACE! Tell men what God did before you tell men what to do! GOD . . . CHRIST . . . *GRACE!* All is to the glory of God; there is nothing in which man can boast. The Gospel is so great, so comprehensive, so all-embracing that it is beyond the grasp of mortal mind. "For God so loved the world, that he gave his only begotten Son, that whosoever believeth in him should not perish, but have everlasting life" (Jn. 3:16). "But God commendeth his love toward us, in that, while we were yet sinners, Christ died for us" (Rom. 5:8). There was a cross in the heart of God before there was a cross at Calvary. God does not love us because we are valuable; we are valuable because God loves us. God does not love us because we are somebody; we are somebody because God loves us! All is grace! GRACE! God's riches at Christ's expense. The Christian Life is grace, and grace is the Christian Life.

Satan attacks men via bribes and threats. Check it out. Read Genesis 3 with Adam and Eve. Read Matthew 4 with Jesus. When Satan cannot bribe he will intimidate. God works with love and trust. He loves men; He trusts men. Evangelism is love and trust. He loves men; He trusts men. Evangelism is love and trust. We must not resort to manipulation. Sinners cannot be "scared into heaven." God must not be presented as merely a "Heavenly Santa Claus." Men are autonomous; "whatsoever will may come." Equally true, "Whatsoever will, may go." Read John 6. Christianity does not externally control others. Faith gives God the glory because Christ is the Savior. God alone can save; God alone can keep (1 Pet. 1:5). The control theme in scripture is promise, prophecy, and the fulfilment is salvation through Jesus Christ. "For I am not ashamed of the gospel of Christ: for it is the power of God unto salvation to everyone that believeth; to the Jew first, and also to the Greek. For therein is the righteousness of God revealed from faith to faith: as it is written, the just shall live by faith" (Rom. 1:16,17). We are saved by grace; don't you ever forget it.

Gifts, Gift, And "The Gift"

There are spiritual gifts (Rom. 12, 1 Cor. 12). There is the gift of the Holy Spirit (Acts 2:38). This is not our issue. This lesson focuses upon and glories in "The Gift." "Thanks be unto God for his unspeakable gift" (2 Cor. 9:15). There are gifts, gift; then there is "The Gift." "The Gift" is Christ. "But God, who is rich in mercy, for his great love wherewith he loved us" (Eph. 2:4). "That in ages to come he might shew the exceeding riches of his grace in his kindness toward us through Christ Jesus" (Eph. 2:7). "Unto me, who am less than the least of all saints, is this grace given, that I should preach among the Gentiles the unsearchable riches of Christ" (Eph. 3:8). "In whom we have redemption through his blood, the forgiveness of sins, according to the riches of his grace" (Eph. 1:7). God in Christ acted once and for all to save man. "Who needeth not daily, as those high priests, to offer up sacrifice, first for his own sins, and then for the people's: for this he did once (and for all), when he offered up himself" (Heb. 9:27). God's grace is centered in "The Gift" . . . Jesus Christ.

Grace And Truth In Jesus Christ

"And the Word was made flesh, and dwelt among us, (and we beheld his glory), the glory as of the only begotten of the Father, full of grace and truth . . . and of his fulness have all received, and grace for grace. For the law was given by Moses, but grace and truth came by Jesus Christ" (Jn. 1:14-17). Familiar verses have to be read more closely. This verse has been misunderstood and mistaught. Some conclude that the law of Moses was without grace . . . that grace began with

50

Jesus. This is not what this verse teaches. Moses was sent by grace; grace revealed the law. This was the will of God. But Moses, himself, was not grace. The law is not grace. Christ is grace! Notice what this text says, "grace and truth." There was truth in Moses, in the law. But Moses was not truth. Jesus is *BOTH* grace and truth. He is the totality, the embodiment of grace and truth. Moses and the law prepared for Jesus. Everything focuses upon Jesus. *CHRIST — CHRIST — CHRIST!* Grace is always incarnated. Grace was incarnate in Christ. Moses gave a message; Christ is "The Message." The emphasis in Christianity is the person and work of Jesus Christ. This is our soil and substance, "To wit, that God was in Christ, reconciling the world unto himself, not imputing their trespasses unto them; and hath committed to us the word of reconciliation" (2 Cor. 5:19).

A pilot was flying on instruments (IFR) in a blinding fog. The radar operator assisted his approach. The pilot, having done his homework, remembered a tower in his path. He yelled this fact out to the control tower. The operator answered calmly, "You obey instructions; we will take care of obstructions." This is the great reality of Christ. He is our everything. Our all in all. He can be trusted. "Trust and obey." In Christ, God is the "Banker of Our Life."

The conclusion is obvious . . . "The Gift" is God Himself! Shout it from the housetop! Christianity is a "God the Father" religion. To see Christ is to have God, and Jesus Christ whom thou has sent" (Jn. 17:3). God gives gifts; but the greatest gift is God Himself. The temptation is to want gifts from God rather than God. We would rather receive salvation from God than "God-our-salvation." This is not semantics! Everything comes from, out-of, "The Gift." Heaven is not merely a gift from God; heaven is God. We will be where He is, as He is. "The Gift" is God in Christ. This eliminates self-reliance. This eliminates the human pride of "paying our own way." Everything is based upon "The Gift." What a relief! We do not have to earn our salvation! Jesus Christ did that for us. He came to save us who cannot save ourselves. Paul, the chiefest sinner, exclaimed, "Thanks be unto God for his unspeakable gift."

Christ Our Salvation

God's gift in Christ is the remission of our sins (1 Cor. 15:1-3). "But he was wounded for our transgressions, he was bruised for our iniquities: the chastisement of our peace was upon him; and with his stripes we are healed" (1 Pet. 1:18,19). "Who his own self bore our sins in his own body on the tree, that we, being dead to sins, should live unto righteousness; by whose stripes ye were healed" (1 Pet. 2:24). "But not as the offence, so also is the free gift. For if through the offence of one many be dead, much more the grace of God, which is by one man, Jesus Christ, hath abounded unto many . . . For if by one man's offence death reigned by one; much more they which receive abundance of grace and of the gift of righteousness shall reign in life by one, Jesus Christ . . . But where sin abounded, grace did much more abound: That as sin hath reigned unto death, even so might grace reign through righteousness unto eternal life by Jesus Christ our Lord" (Rom. 5:16-21). "For when we were yet without strength, in due time Christ died for the ungodly" (Rom. 5:6). Heaven gave all— its most precious jewel—Jesus Christ the Son! "What shall we say then to these things? If God be for us, who can be against us? He that spared not his own Son, but delivered him up for us all, how shall he not with him also freely give us all things?" (Rom. 8:31,32). "Thanks be unto God for his unspeakable gift."

Christ Our Righteousness

Salvation was the godly for the ungodly. Our personal righteousness is that of filthy rags (Isa. 64:6). His righteousness is acceptable to God. His righteousness is my righteousness. Paul went great lengths in Romans to emphasize righteousness as a free gift of God by Christ. Thirty-five times Paul enforces righteousness that cannot be attained by human effort. "Even the righteousness of God which is by faith of Jesus Christ unto all and upon all them that believe: for there is no difference . . . being justified freely by his grace through the redemption that is in Christ Jesus: whom God hath set forth to be a propitiation through faith in his blood, to declare his righteousness for the redemption of sins that are past, through the forbearance of God; to declare, I say, at this time his righteousness: that he might be just, and the justifier of him which believeth in Jesus. Where is boasting then? It is excluded. By what law? of works? Nay: but by the law of faith" (Rom. 3:21-31). "And he found in him, not having mine own righteousness, which is the law, but that which is through the faith of Christ, the righteousness which is of God by faith" (Phil. 3:9). "And he is the propitiation for our sins: and not for ours only, but also for the sins of the world" (1 Jn. 2:2). "But after that the kindness and love of God our Savior toward man appeared, not by works of righteousness which we have done, but according to his mercy he saved us, by the washing of regeneration, and renewing of the Holy Ghost; which he shed on us abundantly through Jesus Christ our Saviour; That being justified by his grace, we should be made heirs according to the hope of eternal life" (Tit. 3:4-7). "Thanks be unto God for his unspeakable gift."

Christ Our Life

Christ is "The Gift." We have little trouble understanding "The Gift" with salvation. But most think grace ends with salvation! It does not! Why do we have difficulty with grace in the Christian's life? Christ is our salvation; He is also our life. "For ye are dead, and your life is hid with Christ in God. When Christ, who is our life, shall appear, then shall ye also appear with im in glory" (Col. 3:1-4). ". . . I am come that they might have life, and that they might have it more abundantly" (Jn. 10:10). ". . . I am the way, the truth, and the life: no man cometh unto the Father, but by me" (Jn. 14:6). Faith saves; faith sustains. How can one believe in eternal life while doubting abundant life? One must have a vision for daily life. If there is not *here* there will be no *after!* When one expects little from God he will not be disappointed. Assurance in eternal life produces audacity in living the abundant life. We trust God to save us then rely upon our own resources. This is futile! This places us back exactly where we were! Only Christ can live the Christian life. But He can live it in me! Man refuses to be totally dependent upon God. In this definition we all are on grace.

A new life demands a new nature. Nicodemus wanted to know more abstract theology to do more things. Jesus repeatedly told him, "You must be born again." One must have a new nature to live a new life. "Therefore if any man be in Christ, he is a new creature: old things are passed away; behold, all things are become new" (2 Cor. 5:17). Jesus is both the author and finisher of our faith (Heb. 12:2). "Whereby are given unto us exceeding great and precious promises: that by these ye might be partakers of the divine nature, having escaped the corruption that is in the world through lust" (2 Pet. 1:4). The word for life is *zoe*. This is the essence, substance of life. Life is not merely quantity—continuous time. Life is quality. Jesus is the source of life. Life is a gift—not a deserved possession. Life physically is God's gift; life spiritually is God's gift.

Jesus is our power source! All the good in me is the Christ in me. The issue is *INTAKE* not *OUTPUT!* We fret over output. Intake determines output. One cannot put out what he previously has not brought in. The only good in me is the Christ in me. God planned it; God initiated it; God carried it out; God revealed it; God enables it! It is all of God! There is no human source in Christianity. Paul said, "I can do all things through Christ which strengthens me" (Phil. 4:13). "Let this mind be in you, which was also in Christ Jesus" (Phil. 2:5). Therefore only a Christian can act like a Christian. Jesus did it; Jesus motivates us; Jesus enables us! The only permanent motivation in Christianity is the grace of God! Read 1 Cor. 15:10; 2 Cor. 5:14! Christ's love is all I need!

Read John 15. Familiar scripture must be read more closely. The Vine and Branches. This is not self-effort upon the part of a branch. This is not a business transaction made by the vine and branches. The life of a branch is in the vine. Intake determines output. "Abide in me, and I in you. As the branch cannot bear fruit of itself, except it abide in the vine; no more can ye, except ye abide in me. I am the vine, ye are the branches: He that abideth in me and I in him, the same bringeth forth much fruit: for without me ye can do nothing" (Jn.

15:4,5). Read this! It is not self-reliance. We are not left upon our own! Jesus did not say, "Without me you can do a little something." He said, "Nothing." Christianity is not the frustration of self-struggle. Christianity is abiding! Abide in Him, in His word, in His love! Fruit cannot be manufactured. I am as strong as the Christ in me. Fruit comes from the tree. Take care of the tree and the tree will produce the fruit. Will we ever learn?

This is a vital lesson we must learn about evangelism. Read Acts. Read the epistles. There is no organized personal work in the New Testament. No one was praised or criticized for evaluated by their responses. Evangelism is a fruit . . . a fruit of grace! People saved by grace share it! It is not manipulation. One method will not fit all. It is not winning arguments. It is not "right answers to selected questions." Evangelism is a result of grace. Only people who can receive grace can share it. We produce who we are. Grace makes Christians; human effort results in mere proselytism. "Thanks be unto God for his unspeakable gift."

"The Gift" Demands Response

Salvation is a gift . . . a free gift. Jesus paid it all. Salvation is a reality. This is the Gospel. Salvation is not a business transaction; salvation cannot be bought, earned, deserved. However, the fact of gift implies acceptance. "The Gift" is not universalism. A gift is received, accepted, appropriated, Jesus is the Great Physician. His advice must be heard; His medicine must be taken. Medicine cannot cure as long as it remains in the bottle on the shelf. One does not obey to secure God's love. The motivation is grace. There have always been two false concepts of salvation: (1) Man can earn his salvation. (2) Man has nothing to do with his salvation. Both are totally wrong. "For we are his workmanship, created in Christ Jesus unto good works, which God hath before ordained that we should walk in them" (Eph. 2:8-10). Grace creates good works. Grace motivates acceptance. "He that believeth and is baptized shall be saved" (Mk. 16:15,16). Works coming from grace eliminates human boasting. All is to the glory of God.

Yes, for all these do I give thanks!
For heart to share, desire to bear,
and will to live.

Flamed unto one by deathless love—
Thanks be to God for this!
Unspeakable! His Gift!

Questions

1. Discuss, again, the profound greatness of grace. Check it out. Have our lessons fortified grace? Is grace becoming sweeter—of more value?
2. How does Satan operate? How does God operate? How do we operate? More like Satan or God?
3. What is the "Gift"? Do we really grasp the depths of the "Gift"?
4. Discuss Jesus as grace and truth.
5. Discuss flying on instruments.
6. Discuss Jesus as our salvation, our righteousness.
7. Discuss in depth Jesus as our life.
8. Discuss intake and output further.
9. Discuss our response.

LESSON 8

The Value Of Grace

Introduction

AMAZING GRACE! Tell men what God did before you
tell men what to do. Christianity is intake not output. Bring
in grace, Christ, be filled with the Spirit. Intake determines
output. *TEST TIME!* Are you ready? Were you profoundly
interested in a study of grace? Were you excited about it?
indifferent? against it? After these lessons what is your attitude? Are you still negative about grace? fearful? squeamish?
Do you still consider grace dangerous? Are you still on the
defensive? Are you interested in grace or, rather, interested
in making sure grace is clearly explained with works? Can you
be comfortable with grace? relaxed? Are you thrilled to study
about God and glorifying Jesus? Do you make sure the glory
is to God? Have you changed your concept of Christianity?
Is it of faith or self-reliance? Will you now focus upon intake
or will you still emphasize output? Can you fellowship someone
who focuses upon grace? Can you stress what God did/does?
Peter said, "But grow in grace, and in the knowledge of our
Lord and Saviour Jesus Christ. To him be glory both now and
forever. Amen" (2 Pet. 3:18). Are you growing in grace? Do
you now have Christ more and more? Are you living by faith?
or by human works? Can you sing "Blessed Assurance"
without having your fingers crossed? Are you glad to be a
Christian? Can you say "Jesus" without mumbling? We are
saved by grace; don't you ever forget it.

Grace Provides Salvation

So many things can be accepted mentally that are still

different to accept emotionally. Sinners are saved by grace! This we mentally accept. Yet we then try to earn/deserve it. Self-reliance dies hard. Sin is violation of law. Sin is also the opposite of trusting in God's redemption. Sin is the activity of self-justification rather than God's. From the beginning to the end salvation is all of God's grace and not man's merit! This hits home hard! Human merit is completely ruled out in the victorious Christian life. One hears about Christ—what God did at Calvary. This is the Gospel. One believes (trusts) in this act with all his heart. Dependence is now upon God. One repents because of the goodness of God (Rom. 2:4; 2 Cor. 7:9,10). It is not the badness of man but the goodness of God. One confesses this new "Boss." Jesus is now the Lord of our lives. One puts Jesus on in baptism. Baptism is passive. One does not baptize himself. This physically illustrates complete acceptance of Christ. "For if all are the children of God by faith in Christ Jesus. For as many of you as have been baptized into Christ have put on Christ" (Gal. 3:26,27). The secret of Christianity is not in self-confidence, self-effort, self-determination. The secret in Christianity is looking to Jesus, the author and finisher of our faith (Heb. 12:1,2). Ephesians 2:8-10 eliminates human boasting. How could one brag about receiving/accepting/utilizing a free gift? Why is this so difficult to accept?

When Jesus died at Calvary God forgave our sins—past, present, and future. Chew on this! Digest this! Live this! This is crucial. Some think one obeys then God ponders forgiveness! *SACRILEGE!* Jesus paid it all. There is nothing else even Jesus can do for the remission of sins. "For this is my blood of the New Testament, which is shed for many for the remission of sins" (Mt. 26:28). "But if we walk in the light, as he is in the light, we have fellowship one with another, and the blood of Jesus Christ his Son cleanseth us from all sin" (1 Jn. 1:7). "But God be thanked, that ye were the servants of sin, but ye have obeyed from the heart that form of doctrine which was delivered you. Being then made free from sin, ye became the servants of righteousness" (Rom. 6:14-18). The sin problem is solved . . . forever! At the cross!

When were you saved? Most would give their date of baptism. In most ways this is correct. However, in one way, it is incorrect. We were all saved the day Jesus died for our sins! We were saved at Calvary. Yet this gift has to be accepted; Christ has to be claimed. Salvation is claimed when one puts on Christ in baptism. This attests our faith in Him and not ourselves. Grace demands obedience. It is a disgrace not to accept grace (2 Cor. 6:1; Gal. 2:20,21). We now belong to Christ "lock, stock, and barrel." "For ye are bought with a price: therefore glorify God in your body, and in your spirit, which are God's" (1 Cor. 6:19,20). Grace demands works! Works has no place for grace! Wrath does not drive to grace; the rejection of grace demands wrath. The greatest demand is love, grace, mercy. Grace reigns through righteousness (Rom. 5,6). Grace demands response; otherwise it is useless and ultimately withdrawn. Christ, "The Gift," must not only be accepted, He must be utilized. He is our source, our power, our strength. Gifts are neither to be unused or buried. They are not solely for the joy of the recipient. Grace causes grace, produces more grace. Rights and duties, privileges and services go hand in hand. Grace saves sinners.

Grace Provides More Grace

Grace not only saves sinners; grace also keeps saints. Do not trip over this. Is grace only for sinners? A beloved song says, "O for grace to trust Thee more." Some have contended this is unscripural . . . that God's grace is complete . . . that there is no more. Some change the wording, "O for faith to trust Thee more." Of course this is all legalistic technicalities. One needs "Religious Loop-hole Lawyers" to keep all of us straight. But this attitude illustrates our fear/ignorance of grace for Christian living. After baptism are Christians "back on their own"? This was their problem in the first place! Did God pitch the Bible out of the sky to Christians saying, "Good Luck"? Christianity *begins* in grace, *continues* in grace, and *ends* in grace. Christians are not under law but grace (Rom. 6:14).

Read and re-read scriptures on grace. "And such trust have we through Christ to God-ward: not that we are sufficient of ourselves to think anything as of ourselves; but our sufficiency is of God" (2 Cor. 3:4,5). "Now our Lord Jesus Christ himself, and God, even our father, which hath loved us, and hath given us everlasting consolation and good hope through grace comfort your hearts, and stablish you in every good word and work" (2 Thess. 2:16,17). Grace is not only the power to save, it is also the power to enable. God provides for what He demands. We are "to work out our salvation" (Phil. 2:12), but the strength is God (Phil. 2:13). Grace creates works (Eph. 2:8-10). God furnishes what He begins in the same manner (Phil. 1:6). "But we believe that through the grace of the Lord Jesus Christ we shall be saved, even as they" (Acts 15:11). Grace is the underlying foundation, the whole presupposition of the Christian life. "Wherefore we receiving a kingdom which cannot be moved, let us have grace, whereby we may serve God acceptably with reverence and godly fear" (Heb. 12:28). "And with great power gave the apostles witness of the resurrection of the Lord Jesus; and great grace was upon them all" (Acts 4:33). "Now when the congregation was broken up, many of the Jews and religious proselytes followed Paul and Barnabas: who, speaking to them, persuaded them to continue in the grace of God" (Acts 13:43). Grace is the divine energy of the Christian. God is able to make us able. "And God is able to make all grace abound toward you; that ye, having all sufficiency in all things, may abound to every good work" (2 Cor. 9:8). "And by their prayer for you, which long after you for the exceeding grace of God in you" (2 Cor. 9:14). Christian works originate in grace! The only permanent motivation in Christianity is grace.

Man never outgrows his deep need for God. James promises more grace, daily grace. "But he giveth more grace. Wherefore he saith, God resisteth the proud, but giveth grace unto the humble" (James 4:6). Like manna one cannot live on stale grace. Like the Israelites we must gather the manna of grace daily. Yesterday's grace cannot handle today! Christianity is not religious humanism. Secular humanism is wrong; religious humanism is wrong. Too many Christians are frustrated trying to live Christianity by main strength and awkwardness. Too many believe, "Do your best and God will do the rest." This is blasphemy, but it dies hard. Paul learned that his human weakness was God's opportunity (2 Cor. 12). We all know

Ephesians 4:4-6; but do we know verse 7, "But unto every one of us is given grace according to the measure of the gift of Christ?" Grace saves; grace also enables. This is the value of Grace.

The Cornstalk

Read Ephesians 3:14-21 carefully, prayerfully. This will demonstrate intake not output. Now use your imagination. Imagine a cornstalk. Command this cornstalk to make corn! It cannot! *A CORNSTALK CANNOT MAKE CORN!* Only God can make corn! He bears corn on a cornstalk. This is fruit not works. It is intake not output. A cornstalk, of itself, cannot manufacture corn. A cornstalk will produce in direct proportion to what it has brought in. This is the simple law of nature— intake determines output. The cornstalk brings in to put out. A cornstalk needs soil, water, sun, minerals. The more the better. You do not blame the cornstalk during a drouth. No farmer is angered with a cornstalk during bad conditions. The cornstalk is at the mercy of intake. Put it in and nature will put it out. *SO SIMPLE!*

Intake determines output. But sermons center upon output. We preach guilt and not grace. We cry, "more, more, more." People then try harder. You cannot save people with guilt, fear and hate. This produces frustration. All over the brotherhood brethren live in doom and gloom. Many have "just given up." They tried only to fail! God did not ask you to try—He asked you to believe! He did not send you out on your own—He both enlightens and enables. Christianity is not another self-improvement course! God provides Christ, "The Gift." He is our life. To the degree we bring in we will put out. This is nature. We fail with intake not output. Cornstalks bear corn naturally. You never saw a cornstalk sweat, breathe hard, quit in frustration. Cornstalks don't "work on" cobs one day, kernels the next. Fruit comes naturally, in season. Fruit is on its own time schedule. A cornstalk will put out in direct proportion to what it brought in.

Now read Ephesians 3:14-21. Notice our intake. Paul says we must be strengthened by the Spirit in the inward man! Christianity is the dispensation of the Holy Spirit. Christiantiy is believing in the Holy Spirit. The Holy Spirit is the "Christian's Partner" (Acts 2:38). Christians are commanded "to be filled with the Spirit" (Eph. 5:18). This means "under the control." The "more Spirit" the "more Christianity" we will have. A temple is defined as a building inhabited by God. Christians are the "Temples of God" (1 Cor. 3:16; 6:19,20). This is an amazing thought! Christians are the "Temples of God." This also is foundational. Many great sermons come from Eph. 5:22-32. They are true and needed—the Christian home. But verses 22-32 follow verse 18. Unless one is filled with the Spirit he is not likely to treat his mate as Christ would. Intake determines output.

Paul then says Christians "intake" Christ. The only good in me is the Christ in me. The more Christ in me the stronger I am. ". . . Be strong in the Lord, and in the power of his might" (Eph. 6:10). Christianity is Christ. 164 times Paul uses the phrase "in Christ." Christianity is putting one in Christ then putting Christ into him! God provides Christ! We can have all "Christ" we wish! Our intake will determine our output.

Paul then encourages love. Remember? Familiar texts need to be read more closely. Christians are rooted and grounded in love. Love, to Paul, is not maudlin sentimentality. Love is not magic. Paul says love is stable. The more love one has the more obedient one is: "If ye love me, keep my commandments" (Jn. 14:15). "For this is the love of God, that we keep his commandments; and his commandments are not grievous" (1 Jn. 5:3). Remember? It is God's love for us that produces our love for God (2 Cor. 5:14; 1 Cor. 15:10; 1 Jn. 4:7-11). Hereby perceive we the love of God, because he laid down his life for us: and we ought to lay down our lives for the brethren" (1 Jn. 3:16). Intake determines output.

Paul then offers the total resources of God! *MIND BOG-GLING!* Christians may be filled with the fullness of God! Not merely an ounce! Not some! *ALL!* Christians can have all the God they will intake! Heaven is at their disposal, "Now unto him that is able to do exceeding abundantly above all that we ask or think, according to the power that worketh in us. Unto him be glory in the church by Christ Jesus throughout all ages, world without end. Amen'' (Eph. 3:20,21). God is able to make us able. Intake determines output. This is the value of grace.

Grace Changes Our Hearts

Christianity is more than intellectual; Christianity must not be reduced to sheer logic. Grace is unfathomable. Grace turns human thinking upside-down. Jesus totally frustrated the Pharisees. His teaching baffled the Jews. Turn to Luke 15, "The Prodigal Son." The "Elder Brother" is not some religious "stick-in-the-mud" who needs to be shot! He represents human justice at its best! Human logic fails! The "Elder Son" was not against being humanitarian . . . he was not against some sort of rehabilitation. He was against a "party" . . . making the Prodigal some kind of a hero! The justice of Jesus is not a distributive justice which gives people what they deserve. The justice of Jesus is one of grace. This justice is not justice in tension with mercy, but justice expressed in mercy. Paradoxically, it is only "good people" that cannot understand/tolerate such justice. As the little boy said, "It ain't right!" Jesus said, "The first is last and the last is first." This bothers us.

Jesus' actions outraged even more than His teachings. "And the Pharisees and scribes murmured, saying, "This man receiveth sinners, and eateth with them" (Luke 15:2). Jesus "chose" to associate with the wrong folks! This included shepherds who could not keep all the ceremonial rituals. This included Gentiles who were not adequately instructed on the law. This included tax-collectors who were renegade, women who did not count, and immoral sinners. Jesus died outside the camp (Heb. 13:12-14). Jesus identified Himself, not with the learned Rabbis, but with the oppressed, depressed, and suppressed. He truly was a friend of sinners.

This is why Matthew 25 shocks us! In His "Judgment Parables" Jesus reveals a judgment different from what we imagine. Those who "have the truth" and are "God's favorites" are found condemned. The judgement is not "right answers to selected questions." The judgement involves benevolence, mercy, and compassion. Matthew 25 makes us uncomfortable! People want simple, tidy, logical explanations. Mercy defies logic. Jesus gives precedence to people "too evil" over folks that are "too good." Grace has value—it changes our entire thinking about God, life, and the judgment.

God hath not promised skies always blue,
Flowers-strewn pathways all our skies through.
God hath not promised sun without rain;
Joy without sorrow, peace without pain.
God hath not promised we shall not know
Toil and temptation, trouble and woe.

He hath not told us we shall not bear,
Many a burden, many a care.
But God hath promised strength for the day,
Rest for the labor, light for the way,
Grace for the trials, help from above,
Unfainting sympathy, undying love.
                                    Author Unknown

Questions

1. Test time? Take the evaluation questions? Is grace now acceptable? developing?
2. Were we saved at the cross or in the baptistry? Discuss how we accepted our salvation at the cross in the baptistry.
3. Is grace continuous? Do Christians have daily grace? Do Christians need grace just as sinners need grace? Are we really thankful for daily grace?
4. Discuss in detail the illustration of the Cornstalk . . . intake versus output.
5. Discuss in-depth Eph. 3:14-19.
6. Is your religion basically mental? Is it religious law?
7. Discuss the "injustice" the Father displayed in forgiving the prodigal. Can you grasp mercy? Extend it to others?

LESSON 9

Anger With Grace

Introduction

AMAZING GRACE! Tell men what God did before you tell men what to do. The unique and pivotal claim of Christianity is that Jesus, the Christ, is the Savior, the one and only Savior of the world. Christianity must not be reduced to philosophy; Christianity is not one of the "comparative religions." "I am the way, the truth, and the life: no man cometh unto the Father, but by me" (Jn. 14:6). "Neither is there salvation in any other: for there is none other name under heaven given among men, whereby we must be saved" (Acts 4:12). Jesus is not just the "best teacher," the "master moralist" . . . Jesus is the Savior who redeemed mankind at Calvary. Jesus is the "Grace Gift" of God that justifies man damned in sin. *GRACE.*

All of us are familiar with the classic TV commercial done by John Houseman, "They make money the old-fashioned way—they earn it." Tragically, many religionists feel this way about salvation—they have earned it! Are you comfortable with grace? Or does grace bother you? Are you more comfortable with *law* or *grace? logic* or *mercy?* Are you troubled with God's grace? If God's grace does bother you, is it because you really don't think you have needed it? Are you afraid to dispense grace to those who do? Grace that is begrudged is not grace . . . it is religious snobbery. Jesus visited over at Simon's house in Luke 7. Simon the Pharisee found his blood pressure rising through the roof—why doesn't Jesus run this harlot away? Simon could not grasp grace. Jesus said, "Her sins, which are many, are forgiven; for she loved much: but to whom little is forgiven, the same loveth little" (Luke 7:47).

Are you afraid of grace but not works? Do you enjoy sermons on mercy? Or does it bother you? When grace is mentioned must it be explained in minute detail? Are you on the defensive. Are you mad with God? Are you angry with grace? We are saved by grace; don't you ever forget it!

You must read Mt. 20:1-16. Familiar verses must be read more closely. Jesus taught the "Parable of the Householder." Some worked all day; some most of the day; some very little. They all received the same pay! Those who worked the most demonstrated—they put up picket lines—they allowed their anger to go into orbit. This parable is so improbable—we would not believe it if Jesus had not told it! The workers said, "It ain't right," "It isn't fair." "It is criminal, unjust, mean." They were not about to stand for it. Basically, they were mad with God! They were angry with grace! This shocks us! The standard of man is not the justice of God! So grace is explained . . . and explained . . . and explained . . . and explained away. Grace is the way God is! This truth is not new! Jonah revealed the same God—and grace.

Jonah

Jonah! The problem prophet! Enigmatic Jonah. What does a Bible student do with Jonah? Yet the entire ministry of Jesus is based upon Jonah. "An evil and adulterous generation seeketh after a sign; and there shall no sign be given to it, but the sign of the prophet Jonah: for as Jonah was three days and three nights in the whale's belly; so shall the Son of man be three days and three nights in the heart of the earth" (Mt. 12:38-41; Luke 11:29-32). Jonah was a sign unto the Ninevites. Several things are obvious: (1) Jesus believed in the historical Jonah! He believed in the "Fish Story." Jesus accepted the Old Testament, God, and miracles. (2) The critical Jews had not done their homework (or they were dishonest). They said no prophet had come from Galilee (Jn. 7:52). Jonah was from Galilee! About six miles from Nazareth. (3) Jesus identified with Jonah being from Galilee—and being three days and three nights. Perhaps also the acid from the stomach of the fish had bleached-out Jonah! What a sight he must have been to those in Ninevah. (4) Grace is revealed in the Old Testament. Jonah and Hosea totally focus upon the grace of God. Men have always had a problem with God, with grace, with mercy. It is much easier to "earn it."

JONAH! GRACE! Yet men are so fascinated about the "Great Fish" they have failed to see the "Great God." Too many cannot see farther than the fish. Jonah, the prophet, was sent to Ninevah to condemn the city. The wicked, vile city of Ninevah! Anything they received, they deserved. Jonah should have gone with joy! The Jews especially hated the Ninevites! Many years previously the Ninevites had murdered Jewish men and assaulted Jewish women. The Ninevite deserved a holocaust! Jonah was privileged to proclaim this justice! But he ran—the other way! Why? Not because he liked the Ninevite! Not because he wished them spared! Jonah knew the heart of God—mercy! Jonah had to protect God! Jonah had to abort grace. Jonah ran! "But it displeased Jonah exceedingly, and he was very angry. And he prayed unto the Lord, and said, I pray thee, O Lord, was not this my saying when I was yet in my country? Therefore I fled into Tarshish: for I knew that thou are a gracious God, and merciful, slow to anger, and of great kindness, and repentest thee of the evil. Therefore now, O Lord, I beseech thee, take my life from me; for it is better for me to die than to live. Then said the Lord, Doest thou well to be angry?" (Jonah 4:1-4). Jonah was angry with grace! Jonah is unable to forgive God for His goodness! Jonah presumed to tell God how to dispense His grace! *I CANNOT BELIEVE IT!* But is there a little Jonah in all of us!?!

So Jonah ran! Although he wanted Ninevah to "go up in smoke" he feared God's compassion. You know the story . . . the storm, the sailors, the fish. Jonah was then willing to go preach—but he still had not learned/accepted grace! This is the whole problem with grace! People that need it don't deserve it! Jonah could condemn Ninevah! He could demand his own death . . . but he totally refused to wrestle with grace! It was God's grace that rescued him from the fish! Jonah could accept grace for himself but not for others. Gilbert Thomas said:

I could not face the scourge of God's forgiveness.
I could bear, amid the world's red guilt and black despair,

They wrath, I cried, but not thy mercy, Lord.
O spare me from the world's unfolding grace,
When every flower is as a two-edged sword.

Are we like Jonah? Can we understand hell but not heaven? Had we rather hear sermons on hell than grace? Are we ready for grace? Jonah was mad, then hard, then stubborn.

Jonah needed Nineveh—not to narrow him, but widen him! He must get out of his bigoted rut—to be more intellectually daring and emotionally expanded. Jonah feared thought, honesty, mercy. At least if Ninevah is saved it must become Jewish. Nineveh must bow to Jerusalem. Nineveh must be circumcised and keep the Sabbath. Ninevah must satisfy man before it can satisfy God! It is more difficult to please men than God. Jonah refused to walk in the depths of grace. Jonah refused to accept the broader confines of God's grace. Israel is not for Israel, but for the world! This is why Jonah is such a keystone of the prophets. He was to call Israel back to her response to Nineveh—"to the remaining world." God is saying to man, "All I want to do is to love you. I want my love received." God does not wish to punish. God wants to save, to heal, to restore, to bless! In whatever man does without God he will fail miserably or succeed even more miserably! Jonah makes all preachers turn green with envy with his responses! Yet he was incensed. He wanted punishment not salvation. He had turned "Good News" into "Bad News." From ship to shore to the suburbs Jonah had fought grace. Now he pens the saddest words in scripture. "Death is better to me than life." Jonah's world was too neat, clean, and tidy to be altered by grace. Jonah was angry with grace. Let God be God!

The Elder Brother

Read Luke 15. The Pharisees were angered with Jesus—He received sinners! They were angry with grace. Luke 15 is Jesus' sermon on grace . . . the Lost Sheep, the Lost Coin, the Lost Boy. The Prodigal returns! If God had "horse-whipped" him, put him on probation, demanded penance! The trouble with

God is—He simply forgave him. The Elder Son goes into a rage! He is blinded to his own blessings. He judges his baby brother with suspicions. The Father that "ran" to meet the Prodigal "walked" out into the night to plead with the Elder Son. The Elder Son did not "need grace" nor did he want grace. He would not allow others to receive it. He attacked God the Father via the Prodigal Son. The Elder Son was angry with grace. The Prodigal Son accepted grace; the Elder Son rejected it. Grace will be the determining issue in the judgment! Are you nervous with grace? Do you try to control grace? Have you turned grace into law? Do you tell God to whom He can dispense grace? Do you have trouble with God? Let God be God!

The Trouble With God Is

Return to Mt. 20. The "all day workers" were angered. Notice (1) No one was cheated. The "last workers" were not paid at the expense of the "early workers." The "bonus" had not come at the expense of the "salary" of others. All were paid. (2) It was not the workers business how the "Boss" spent his money. They made a deal and were paid accordingly. Why develop ulcers trying to equalize the world? God has not ask us to straighten out the world. God never told us the world would be "fair in our eyes"! The Potter has power over the clay; employers have the right to run their own businesses. (3) The "Boss" made a contract. There is no communism in Mt. 20! The "Boss" signed the contract; the "Boss" had a right to be generous. (4) The "Early Group" made a deal; the "Last Group" relied upon trust. The first group got so much pay for so much work. They received theirs. The others trusted the "Boss." God rewards trust.

Then why were the workers mad? They were angry with generosity. They were mad with grace. Had they been mistreated? No. It was God's generosity to others that angered them. Let God be God! Don't try to force God into our way of thinking. The early workers had forgotten to be thankful that they had a job! They also did not grasp the privilege of service. "Death-bed repentance" bothers us! Why? Are we jealous? Would we actually wish to sin all of our lives then repent the last minute? Is this our real wish? Jesus forgave the "Thief on the Cross" (Luke 23). Some even deny the Thief was saved! Why this interpretation? Because it smacks at grace! This frightens us! We cannot allow grace! So the workers never grasped how privileged they were to serve God all their lives. When a young preacher I baptized an elderly man. He had attended services for years and years. We were all so thrilled. Then he explained, "I have little left; I have cheated God and myself." How true! The "last workers" were deprived of the privilege of ministry! All they received was money! Money is the least satisfying commodity on earth. The problem is always grace. Let God be God.

The Pharisee And The Publican

Read Luke 18:9-14. There were two men. One, in so many ways, was a failure. He failed in his marriage, with his children, and in his business. But he did have heart. To a degree his life was partially salvaged. His funeral was enormous! People came and openly cried. This man was loved and trusted. The other man, in so many ways, was successful. He had one wife and no divorce. The children married well. This man was an officer at church. His funeral was small. People did not come nor cry. They neither loved nor trusted him. He could not get along with people.

Now this is not advocating failure over success, evil rather than good. It is saying that our concepts of "good and evil" may not be God's. This is saying there is grace, mercy, and forgiveness. The first man had nothing upon which to glory. He cast himself upon God! Grace produces mercy. Until grace is received mercy cannot be given. A mercy problem is, in reality, a grace issue. This humility eliminated pride, self-righteousness. The first man could receive grace and glory in grace.

The second man trusted himself. "He made religion the old-fashioned way—he earned it." He had no need for God; he had no concept of grace. He was superior, impatient, intolerant. He was cold and hard.

70

Is this not Luke 18! Jesus said, "Two men went to church." The Pharisee was proud of self. He had his little "check list" of things he knew and did. If anyone made it to heaven he would. He was proud he was not weak and sinful like others. So good yet so bad! A denial of grace.

The Publican? He had nothing, claimed nothing, "God, be merciful to me a sinner." He went home justified! Grace! Amazing Grace! Can you accept it? Can you cast yourself upon the grace of God? Are you suspicious, fearful of grace? Are you angry with grace? Are you mad with God? Let God be God!

Questions

1. Is this lesson the most incisive of all? Are we really for it? Can we handle it? Can we admit grace? Can we allow grace? Are we angry with grace?
2. Discuss Jonah in great detail. Are we like Jonah?
3. Discuss the Elder Brother in great detail. Are we more like the Elder Brother than the Prodigal?
4. What, basically, was the difference between the Elder Brother and the Prodigal?
5. Study Mt. 20 in great detail. "The trouble with God is." Were any workers cheated? Was this communism? Was this grace?
6. Discuss the Pharisee and the Publican. How big will your funeral be?

71

Grace Is Gracious

Introduction

AMAZING GRACE! Tell men what God did before you tell men what to do. Salvation is not merely a matter of grace; it is not merely a matter of obedience. Grace causes obedience; the only permanent motivation in Christianity is grace. This is the crucial issue. It is *INTAKE NOT OUTPUT!* Intake determines output. The foundation of obedience is acceptance of grace. Man chafes at this! Man prefers salvation as a business transaction. God paid a part now man pays his part. But salvation is a gift to be received from God in obedience! Therefore Christianity is dependency not sufficiency, trust not self-reliance. Grace is received by a system of faith. Re-read Hebrews 11! Familiar scripture must be read more closely. The great men in Hebrews 11 were not heroes in modern human understanding. They were not demonstrations of self-reliance but faith. It was not what they did but what God did through them by faith! At a point in time *all* were failures! Remember Peter sank! Remember Paul was a murderer! But God claimed them by grace through faith. It was their intake that determined their output.

Again, Hebrews 11. For eighty years Moses had not fulfilled his potential. He was nothing but ashes! Under his power he could only become a murderer. This is the folly of self-reliance. God called Moses in a burning bush. It was not the bush but God in that bush! "Any ole bush will do!" "Any ole man will do" if God is brought in. When Christ is brought in then Christianity comes out! This approach is crucial. Man would rather "go it alone." Re-read 2 Cor. 12:7-10. God's power is demonstrated in human weakness. Paul was strong when he was weak! Our strength is God not us. Everything Paul was came from the power of grace (1 Cor. 15:10). This is humbling—yet awesome.

This is why Christianity is not merely a "modern, spruced-up Law of Moses." Listen to Jesus, "No man putteth a piece of new cloth unto an old garment . . . neither do men put new wine into old bottles: else the bottles break, and the wine runneth out, and the bottles perish: But they put new wine into new bottles, and both are preserved" (Mt. 9:16,17). Grace-righteousness is not self-righteousness. Pharisees always stumble over grace! They consider themselves an "asset" to God! God is blessed in having them! They also consider themselves better than others. One proud lady prayed, "God grant me grace to stand people another day!" What a mis-concept of grace! Grace is real only when sin is real! Real sinners grasp real grace. He that is forgiven little loves little (Luke 7). Many cannot appreciate grace because they are not profoundly convicted of sin. Grace is not the third line of a syllogism! Creedalists are far more comfortable with law than grace, logic than mercy. The Pharisee prayed, "I thank thee, that I am not as other men are" (Luke 18:11). This man's perverted religion shocks us! It should! The Elder Son (Luke 15) rejected grace. He would have no part in it! He shocks us too! Grace is gracious. We are saved by grace; don't you ever forget it.

God Is Gracious

Grace makes one gracious. This is obvious and automatic. Jonah tried to protect God because he knew God was gracious (Jonah 4:2). The Bible repeatedly says, "God who is rich in mercy." Paul was saved by mercy (1 Tim. 1:12-16). Many misunderstood the prophets. They would reduce them to men who were delighted to preach God's condemnation. The prophets did condemn; but the bottom line was not a "mean ole God" but a God who was saying, "All I want to do is love you." God's love being abused results in wrath! Grace demands wrath! But grace produces mercy! Peter said God is gracious, "If so be ye have tasted that the Lord is gracious" (1 Pet. 2:3). Grace is gracious.

74

The best things are nearest:
breath in our nostrils,
light in your eyes,
flowers at your feet,
duties at your hand,
the path of God just before you.
—Robert Louis Stevenson

Jesus is our model (1 Pet. 2:21). But if He only is our model then no one can believe Him. Only when He is our sacrifice then all can believe (1 Tim. 1:12-16). Jesus being a perfect model can only frustrate me! Jesus being a perfect sacrifice is grace. The conclusion? One must accept Jesus as a gift before they can follow Him as an example! Recipients of grace are gracious! Our problem with mercy is actually grace. He that will not accept grace cannot extend mercy. If there is any truth about Jesus—"He treated people right." *TREAT PEOPLE RIGHT!* Jesus does not make men mean! Jesus does not take advantage of people! Jesus never deceived, manipulated people! Evangelism is grace made gracious. There is an attitude of the Gospel as well as content (Eph. 4:15). Sinners are to be loved and served—not merely "told off"—changed Christian lives are still the greatest impact upon others. Only when others can see changes in us can there be changes in them.

Christians saved by grace must be gracious. We have been successful in the "strong virtues" . . . work, law, discipline. We have not been successful in the "sweet virtues" . . . common Christian courtesy, thoughtfulness, kindness, forgiveness, understanding, patience, longsuffering. The grace of God enables Christians to be gracious. Forgiveness motivates forgiveness (Mt. 6; Eph. 4). "But go ye and learn what that meaneth. I will have mercy, and not sacrifice: for I am not come to call the righteous, but sinners to repentance" (Mt. 9:13). "Woe unto you, scribes and Pharisees, hypocrites! For ye pay tithe of mint and anise and cummin and have omitted the weightier matters of the law, judgment, mercy, and faith: these ought ye to have done, and not to leave the other undone" (Mt. 23:23). ". . . Verily I say unto you, That the publicans and the harlots go into the kingdom of God before you" (Mt. 21:32). Frightening language yet needed! Matured Christians

75

are compassionate, kind and good. They are easy to live with! Christianity must not be reduced to "law-letter." Christianity is relationships. Our relationship to God, self, others (Mt. 22:36-40). We must become "good" with relationships. Christian liberty is not a license for selfish sin; it is the power to work out grace in our lives. We have become a child of God by grace. We are to become what we are! This new birth results in new life! "Who hath saved us, and called us with an holy calling, not according to our works, but according to his own purpose and grace, which was given us in Christ Jesus before the world began" (2 Tim. 1:9). "I therefore, the prisoner of the Lord, beseech you that ye walk worthy of the vocation wherewith ye are called" (Eph. 4:1). "Wherefore the rather, brethren, give diligence to make your calling and election sure: for if ye do these things, ye shall never fall" (2 Pet. 1:10). A new nature produces a new life (2 Pet. 1:4). Christians, by grace, must out-think, out-love, and out-live all others! The Jews blasphemed the name of God (Rom. 2). Poor living and grace are contradictions! "May the God of peace make of us what he would have us be through Jesus Christ" (Heb. 13:21). One man succinctly prayed, "I pray that Thy name, O Lord, shall be written in my life." Only a Christian can act like a Christian! Only Jesus can live the Christian life—but He can live it in us! Grace is gracious.

Grace Produces Gratitude

God loves me! Jesus Christ died to be my personal Savior! God justifies the ungodly, the undeserving. Christianity is not a question of grim duty but a generous gift (2 Cor. 9:15). The grace of God does not call us out of misery into more misery, out of gloom into more gloom. We must not preach "Gospel" to sinners and "grit" to Christians. Joy, not grit, is the hallmark Christian virtue. Grace produces gratitude. Gratitude from the sheer, unreserved, extravagant, generosity of an ever-giving God! *GRACE! GRATITUDE!* The outgoing of God to persons is grace; the outgoing of persons to God is faith. Do we find it difficult—yea impossible—to trust our salvation to God's grace?

The key to life is gratitude. The "Mother Virtue" is gratitude. The opposite of pride is not humility; the opposite of pride is gratitude. Gratitude is the mother of humility. One is always humbled before the ones indebted!

O love that will not let me go—
I give Thee back the life I owe.

We work *FROM* the gift not *TO* it! Christianity begins with the gift. One cannot be grateful for nothing; one cannot be grateful to no one! Now the catch! One cannot be grateful for a gift if one is not willing or eager to be in a relation of loving dependence upon the giver. Gratitude is more than appreciation; gratitude is humbled dependence. We accept the gifts because we need "The Giver." In fact, we accept "The Giver." To enthusiastically accept the gifts is to trust ourselves to the Giver! This is our difficulty. We wish the gifts but not to be dependent upon God for it! Man does not wish to be obligated! We want gifts; we are less than enthusiastic about receiving them from God! Some of us even reduce salvation to an "Insurance Plan." "I will give myself to a worldly life, but just in case something goes wrong, I'll make my peace with Jesus." *BLASPHEMY!* Christ is the "Pearl of Great Price." He is *ALL* or *NOTHING!* God was not just *near* us *beside* us. He did not merely send "gifts." God became *ONE* of us. Read Matthew 1. Jesus is "God with us." God did not merely sympathize with us from a distance; He didn't send flowers to the hospital. Jesus is God incarnate (Jn. 1, Phil. 2). Jesus accepted the pains of life for us. He died for us. That is why the Gospel is bascially "Good News." It is redemption from sin and death; it is a new status (Rom. 8). When one sees the Gospel under these terms then he sees himself as the recipient of this undeserved gift of eternal life, and sees God as the absolute benefactor. This is gratitude! The two consequences are a sense of blessing and a sense of absolute dependency.

One with gratitude in Jesus sees himself radically and constantly blessed, accepted and important in the Beloved (Eph. 1:6,7). Gratitude not only is a sense of absolute dependency, but also a sense of spiritual well-being! Being humbled allows one to be exalted! So gratitude enables one the self-confidence to be compassionate. Being secured at the center one can live at the circumference. Gratitude is the joyous acceptance of grace—"The Gift." It is the healthy being at one with myself as poor, weak, unworthy yet saved! Real gratitude causes real humility which guarantees real compassion. Grace makes one gracious.

Blessed Assurance

Anyman, anywhere at anytime can go to hell! A believer can cease believing; one saved can become lost. "Once saved, always saved" is error. The inability of apostasy is error. Eternal security is wrong; but eternal insecurity is equally wrong! God does not want His children to live in guilt but grace! Can one live in uncertainty? Is uncertainty better than certainty? Is one to be driven to heaven by fear or led there by love? Can you tell a sinner with certainty he is lost? How? By scripture! Can you tell a believer he is saved? How? By scripture. "And this is the record, that God hath given to us eternal life, and this life is in his Son. He that hath the Son hath life; and he that hath not the Son of God hath not life. These things have I written unto you that believe in the name of the Son of God; that ye may know that ye have eternal life, and that ye may believe on the name of the Son of God" (1 Jn. 5:11-13). "And this is life eternal, that they might know thee the only true God, and Jesus Christ whom thou has sent" (Jn. 17:3). "There is therefore now no condemnation to them which are in Christ Jesus who walk not after the flesh, but after the Spirit" (Rom. 8:1).

Do you believe a penitent baptized sinner is saved 10 minutes after baptism? Then why not 10 years later? If God can keep a man 10 minutes why not 10 years? After baptism is it all down hill? Would it be wise to "shoot" folks in the baptistry? Do we believe in baptism in Christ? Read 1 Cor. 1:17! Christians must have the joy of assurance! It is a crime to steal joy from Christians! BEWARE OF "JOY-ROBBERS"! Do not turn the "Good News" (Gospel) into "Bad News." Jesus Christ is the Savior; the church is the "saved." The "Church must act like it." Put on the "Helmet of Salvation" before you use the "sword of the Spirit" (Eph. 6:17). Christians cannot be "soul winners bare-headed." We sing "Blessed Assurance, Jesus Is Mine." Is our singing better than our preaching?

At a Youth Rally teens were asked about their knowledge of their spiritual condition. These are "our best." 12% believed they were saved; 33% believed they were lost; 55% simply did not know! This indicts us! What can one uncertain offer a sinner? Can we give him something we don't have? Can he be saved when we are not? Do Christians "die with their fingers-crossed"? One cannot "assure" who is "not sure." God cannot use a man who doubts his conversion. God can do nothing with a Church that fails to understand assurance!

Salvation cannot be based upon human effort. There is always something I do not know and something I have not done. One can always know more and do better. Assurance is with grace. Christianity is not "right answers to selected questions"! The judgment will not be determined by our answers to a "religious pop quiz." Assurance is founded in grace, in Christ by faith. A Christian can "sleep with this."

The Aroma Of Christ

The best argument for Christianity is Christians! "The proof of the pudding is in the eating." "For we are unto God a sweet savour of Christ, in them that are saved, and in them that perish" (2 Cor. 2:14-17). Christians are the "perfume" of Christ. Christians are not only the "salt" of the earth but also the "sugar." Only when love is seen will the message be heard (Eph. 4:15). People will only listen when loved. They do not care how much we know until they know how much we care. The first "Bible" people read are Christians. We are epistles known and read by all men (2 Cor. 3:2). Christians are to mature even unto the stature of Christ (Eph. 4:11-16). A beautiful bride (the Church) is the key to evangelism. The Crucified Savior can only be communicated by Crucified Servants! "But we all, with open face beholding as in a glass the glory of the Lord, are changed into the same image from glory to glory, even as by the Spirit of the Lord" (2 Cor. 3:18).

One cannot deliver the message without the ministry!

Evangelism is the spontaneous chattering of good news. It was done naturally, constantly, easily, and joyously by Christians wherever they went. There were not organized personal work programs in Acts! Evangelism is not a program—it is a life! It is who you are—not something you do on Tuesday nights. We cannot have what early Christians had and do what they did without having the power they had! Can you practice what I preach? Can I preach what you practice? Evangelism is not a system; it is a person. Evangelism is bringing others face to face with Jesus through us! We are "ministers of reconciliation" (2 Cor. 5:18-20). Evangelism is sharing the good news of grace—what God has done for all.

Grace Is Gracious

Grace results in grace. "Let your speech be always with grace, seasoned with salt, that ye may know how ye ought to answer every man" (Col. 3:6). "Let all bitterness, and wrath, and anger, and clamour, and evil speaking, be put away from you, with all malice: and be ye kind one to another, tenderhearted, forgiving one another, even as God for Christ's sake hath forgiven you" (Eph. 4:31,32). "Put on, therefore, as the elect of God, holy and beloved, bowels of mercies, kindness, humbleness of mind, meekness, longsuffering; forbearing one another, if any man have a quarrel against any: even as Christ forgave you, so also do ye. And above all these things put on charity, which is the bond of perfectness. And let the peace of God rule in your hearts" (Col. 3:12-15).

To Risk

To laugh is to risk appearing the fool.
To weep is to risk appearing sentimental.
To reach out for another is to risk involvement.
To place your ideas, your dreams before the
    crowd is to risk their loss.
To love is to risk not being love in return.
To live is to risk dying.
To hope is to risk despair.
To try is to risk failure.

But risk must be taken, because the greatest hazard in life is to risk nothing. The person who risks nothing, does nothing, has nothing and is nothing. He may avoid suffering and sorrow, but he simply cannot learn, grow, feel change, love, live. Chained by his certitudes, he is a slave, he has forfeited freedom. Only a person who risks is free.

—Author Unknown

Questions

1. Discuss Hebrews 11. How were the heroes failures until God used them by grace?
2. Does grace make one gracious? Are you gracious?
3. Discuss "Treat People Right."
4. Discuss how many are "good" with the strong virtues yet weak with the sweet virtues.
5. Discuss gratitude in great detail. Is it easy for man to be dependent? Discuss gratitude in the context of health.
6. Discuss blessed assurance. How many present are saved? Must Christians be assured? Or is uncertainty part of orthodoxy?
7. Discuss Christians as the aroma of Jesus.

Grow In Grace

Introduction

AMAZING GRACE! Tell men what God did before you tell men what to do. The only permanent motivation in Christianity is the grace of God. Bring men to the cross; keep men at the cross. Everything in Christianity comes from the soil of grace. There are "gifts of grace"; there is also "The Gift" (2 Cor. 9:15). Christ is "The Gift." Christianity is Christ! "The Gift" purchased but one thing—the church! The result of grace is the church! The privileges/benefits of grace are found in the grace-body—the church! You cannot separate grace—Christ—the Church. "Take heed therefore unto yourselves, and to all the flock, over the which the Holy Ghost hath made you overseers, to feed the Church of God, which he hath purchased with his own blood" (Acts 20:28). "Husbands, love your wives, even as Christ also loved the church, and gave himself for it; That he might sanctify and cleanse it with the washing of water by the word, that he might present it to himself a glorious church, not having spot, or wrinkle, or any such thing; but that it should be holy and without blemish" (Eph. 5:25-27). "Unto him be glory in the church by Christ Jesus throughout all ages, world without end. Amen" (Eph. 3:21).

To believe in grace is to love His Church. "And I say also unto thee, That thou art Peter, and upon this rock I will build my church; and the gates of hell shall not prevail against it" (Mt. 16:18). Familiar scripture must be read more closely. Notice what Jesus did not say. (1) "I will build *YOUR* church." He built His church! This is basic. Some make the Church their own private property. It is easy for preachers and elders to fall into this trap. They believe the church is uniquely theirs. Decisions are made on their likes and dislikes. Prayer to God is "for their projects" not the will of God. Such become frustrated yea bitter when their plans fail! Jesus did not build "our" church! Grace produced His! (2) *YOU* will build my church." This results in misguided zeal. This really creates problems. A young man wants to preach so badly—but he is a catastrophy. We need missionaries—but only the ones God sends! Neurotic zeal is a tragedy. Zealous "Church Workers" try to build "Christ's Church" with their own power. This, too, is calamity. Members are assigned guilt and fear. For a time a congregation grows under frantic works. Then "the wheels come off" and the dominoes all fall down." Then God receives the blame. Jesus built His Church! We do not! Christianity is trust-worthy grace not self-effort. Christianity is dependency not self-reliance. The Church is where God's grace-works are done (Eph. 2). Grace is through faith. When one fails in his Christian life it is usually because he has never received anything from God. The only sign a Christian has is to know he has received something from Jesus. We must accept our acceptance.

Our jargon betrays us. Good members are titled, "Good Church Workers." Christians are workers (2 Cor. 6:1; 1 Cor. 3:9). However scripture never uses the term "Good Church Worker." Christians and "Good Church Worker" may not be synonymous terms. It is much easier to do something for God than to trust God.

> Rock of ages, cleft for me,
> Let me hide myself in Thee.
> Let the water and the blood
> From Thy wounded side which flowed.
> Be of sin the double cure,
> Save from wrath and make me pure.

Every virtue we possess belongs to Christ alone. It is not what we do for Christ that matters—it is what we let Him do in and through and by us. Satan does not have to make good men bad or bad men worse. All Satan needs is to make men good without Christ! The Christian's problem is to concentrate upon Christ. Christians slander God when they try to do great things

FOR Him without any interest in *KNOWING* Him! Christianity is a "God" religion. The grace of yesterday is not sufficient for today! Jesus told us to pray for daily bread (Mt. 6). This is daily grace.

> Nothing in my hand I bring;
> Simply to Thy cross I cling.

Christianity is Christ! It must not be reduced to "Try harder, more, more, more." We are saved—not because we are good—but because God is! We are saved by grace; don't ever forget it.

Grow In Grace

"But grow in grace, and in the knowledge of our Lord and Saviour Jesus Christ. To him be glory both now and forever. Amen" (2 Pet. 3:18). This is the last line of inspiration from Peter. He tries to say it all . . . "Grow in grace, knowledge, Christ." Notice again it is intake not output! This is dynamite! The final words of an old soldier of the cross, an apostle, disciple, a buddy of Jesus, a preacher, a writer, an elder—the legacy of Peter in one verse! This arrests our attention. What does he say? What "says it all"? *GROW IN GRACE!*

Let us notice what Peter did not say. (1) He did not say, "Let us grow in works." Works did come—but from grace. Peter did not say, "Go to more services, read more chapters, knock on more doors, give more dollars, try harder!" Peter did not promote output. Output develops religious pride . . . attention focuses upon self. "I have more religion than you . . . I do more than you . . . I attend more services than you . . . I speak in more tongues than you." Activity causes one to compare himself with others. Paul condemns this in 2 Cor. 10:12,13. Grace gets one out of the pride business. ". . . knowledge puffeth up, but love edifies" (1 Cor. 8:1). No one, religiously, will ever be "in the black." Grace is freedom from "do-it-yourself religion." Christianity is not "to man be the glory." (2) Peter did not say, "think about yourself." Get your mind off yourself; get yourself off your mind. Christianity centers upon Christ. (3) Peter did not say the judgment would be performance. If the judgment were a religious quiz, then what score would pass? 70? 80? 90? 100? Watch out! One would have to be perfect! Could you make 100? Moderns compare today on a "scale of 1 to 10." A bad guy is 2; a good guy is 5; a real religious guy is 6! Are you a 10? Aren't you glad grace eliminates such foolishness? One legalist allowed 2% error! Where did he get that? Aren't you glad salvation does not depend upon perfect knowledge? perfect performance? There has never been the perfect song, sermon, prayer! By the way, no man has ever "repented perfectly." Some would demand perfect repentance. Anything any man does is flawed! No man is infallible, inspired, or inerrent! The last thing any man gives up is his own autonomy—his own self-suffering.

Why do we keep resisting grace? Read our sermons/articles when others challenge our trust in grace! These articles invariably affirm a faith in grace—but they are 99% about works! Others force us to preach grace! *WHY?* Why be on the defensive? The Bible is not! Peter was not!

This also surfaces another problem. Too many faithful brethren think/feel they have committed the "Unpardonable Sin." The *best* still think the *worst!* This is not the place for a discussion of the "Unpardonable Sin." But the fact of fear illuminates benign neglect in the study and practice of grace. A "works oriented" religion produces fear! It is vital to know what Peter did not emphasize in 2 Peter 3:18.

Now let us notice what Peter does say. (1) Grow in grace. More and more know how much God loves! John 3:16; Romans 5:6-8; 1 John 4:7-11. Grow in Christ, grow in the cross, grow in the Gospel, grow in the price God paid to save me! *PAID IN FULL!* This is what God stamped on Calvary! Sinners by grace enter into the finished work of salvation. God loves me! God wants me! God blesses me! *DWELL ON THIS!* Christians stand upon conquered ground! There are two seas in Palestine. The Sea of Galilee takes in only to put out. It is a living, vibrant sea. The Dead Sea receives but does not put out. It is dead! Grace is the root of all in life that is sweet, lovely, and good. (2) Peter had learned this from experience. Both Peter and Paul were activists. In modern motivational circles they would serve as "success examples." Religion did not come easily. Peter kept "running ahead under his own power." Paul would have murdered every soul on earth to

86

extinguish Christianity. They were self-reliant! But they were converted. Read John 21. Remember familiar scripture has to be read more closely. Three times Jesus presses Peter, "Do you love me?" What is the "bottom line" in said questioning? "Peter, humanly speaking, you think you are 'washed up'." Humanly speaking, you are! But not "Christ-speaking." Peter, will you learn grace, accept forgiveness. Peter did not preach on Pentecost because he had earned the right to! He preached because he knew what all men must know—grace! Grace provides forgiveness. Never put a man into the pulpit who understands not forgiveness! Peter learned grace through bitter tears (Luke 22:62). Judas could not deny self—Peter did!

(3) Peter agreed with Paul about grace. Both Peter and Paul were stumbling activists. They were saved by grace. Paul's favorite word was grace (101 times). Peter built his two epistles upon grace! Like Paul he used the words "grace and peace." Peter was positive—not defensive—about grace! Peter's epistles gave God the glory in Christ! Peter knew by experience that man is saved to glorify God and enjoy God! (4) Peter knew to grow in grace is to grow in dependency. The longer Christians live the more Christians realize their minute-to-minute need of God. Too many reject calling upon God because their problem is either (1) too big or (2) too little! *NONSENSE!* God is our loving Father. Nothing is too giant or trivial! A suggestion. Call it a "game" if you wish. Take an hour—60 minutes. See how many minutes in that hour God is on your mind. Keep adding minutes to that hour. Practice the presence of God. Allow God into every minute of your life. Do not grow merely in knowledge but dependency. "Casting down imaginations, and every high thing that exalteth itself against the knowedge of God, and bringing into captivity every thought to the obedience of Christ; and having in a readiness to revenge and disobedience, when your obedience is fulfilled. Do ye look on things after the outward appearance? If any man trust to himself that he is Christ's, let him of himself think this again, that, as he is Christ's, even so are we Christ's" (2 Cor. 10:5-7). "That I may know him" (Phil. 3:7-10). Christianity is a living, growing, abiding knowledge of God. Not merely knowing about God (facts about God) but knowing God. God the God of all grace! To know God is to accept Grace!

Several Kinds of Grace

We must study our Bibles. We must study grace. Take your concordance and notice the various kinds of grace. Such studies are both interesting and practical. There is "suffering grace." Paul talked about this in 2 Cor. 12 relative with his thorn in the flesh. The grace of God enables during suffering. Don't blame God in tragedy—search for God. There is "singing grace." Happy people sing (James 5:13). One cannot be made to sing out of duty. Paul and Silas sang in a prison (Acts 16:25). Grace produces joy. Joy sings. "Let the word of Christ dwell in you richly in all wisdom; teaching and admonishing one another in psalms and hymns and spiritual songs, singing with grace in your hearts to the Lord. And whatsoever ye do in word or deed, do all in the name of the Lord Jesus, giving thanks to God and the Father by him" (Col. 3:16,16). A singing problem is a grace problem. There is "strengthening grace." "Thou therefore, my son, be strong in the grace that is in Christ Jesus" (2 Tim. 2:1). "And of his fulness have all we received, and grace for grace" (Jn. 1:16). What gives a Christian joy? What motivates a Christian to keep going? What allows a Christian to sleep with peace at night? *GRACE!* What enables one to continue when the road is rough? *GRACE!* "The grace of the Lord Jesus Christ, and the love of God, and the communion of the Holy Ghost, be with you all. Amen" (2 Cor. 13:14).

Grace Teaches

"But grow in grace, and in the *knowledge* of our Lord and Savior Jesus Christ." Love instructs. Grace is practical. As you study the epistles notice the order—doctrine then duty, revelation then responsibility. First tell men what God has done, then what man does in response. "For the grace of God that bringeth salvation hath appeared unto all men. Teaching us that, denying ungodliness and worldly lusts, we should live soberly, righteously, and godly, in the present world" (Tit. 2:11,12). Grace is not magic; grace is not cheap; grace is not careless. Grace renounces that which is wrong and enforces that which is right. This is the instructive nature of grace. Grace enables one to say "no"; grace enables one to say "yes." Grace does not leave one as he was! Nitschze well said, "I will believe in the Redeemer God when I see Him in the lives of the redeemed." Grace cost heaven all heaven had; grace costs us all we have. Grace is free but not cheap. There is no "something-for-nothing" grace. Cheap grace is what we give ourselves; cheap grace is grace without discipleship. "Go ye therefore, and teach (make disciples) of all nations, baptizing them in the name of the Father, and of the Son, and of the Holy Ghost: Teaching them to observe all things whatsoever I have commanded you: and, lo, I am with you always, even unto the end of the world. Amen" (Mt. 28:19,20).

Grace Obeys

Because Christ died by grace we die to self and sin. "Who gave himself for us, that he might redeem us from all iniquity, and purify unto himself a peculiar people, zealous of good works. These things speak, and exhort, and rebuke with all authority. Let no man despise thee" (Tit. 2:14,15). Grace results in grace. We receive grace to be gracious.

God cannot do anything *TO* us or *FOR* us without *US!* Jesus demonstrated to Peter, "Whosoever will may come; whosoever will may go" (Jn. 6). Grace accepts Christ not only as a "Personal Savior" but as a "Personal Lord." Jesus now rules over lives. *OBEY!* Thank God for the difficult things He gives us to do! His salvation is a great thing, but it also is a heroic, holy thing. Grace *TESTS* one for all he is worth! Grace demands! Grace enables! "Verily, verily I say unto you, He that believeth on me, the works that I do shall he do also; and greater works than these shall he do; because I go unto my Father" (Jn. 14:12). ". . . If a man love me, he will keep my words: and my Father will love him, and we will come unto him, and make our abode with him" (Jn. 14:23). "Hereby perceive we the love of God, because he laid down his life for us: and we ought to lay down our lives for the brethren" (1 Jn. 3:16). Grace is tough!

Isaiah saw God in Isaiah 6! The more God he saw the more

sin he saw. The more grace he saw the more obedient be became. "Also I heard the voice of the Lord, saying, whom shall I send, and who will go for us? Then said I, Here am I; send me" (Isa. 6:8). Tell men what God did; then tell men what to do!

Questions

1. Discuss the Church as the "grace-body."
2. Discuss Mt. 16:13-20. Notice what is not said then is said. Discuss the difference between Christians and "Good Church Workers."
3. What were Peter's final words to brethren? What did he not say? What about "guilt trips" among believers? Were Paul and Peter achievers?
4. Discuss the various kinds of grace. Discuss how grace teaches and enables.
5. Discuss how grace causes obedience.

Law Or Grace

Introduction

AMAZING GRACE! Tell men what God did before you tell men what to do. The heart of God was demonstrated at the cross of Calvary. "And as Moses lifted up the serpent in the wilderness, even so must the Son of man be lifted up . . . For God so loved the world, that he gave his only begotten Son, that whosoever believeth in him should not perish, but have everlasting life. For God sent not his Son into the world to condemn the world; but that the world through him might be saved" (Jn. 3:14-17). The "Brass Snake" was a preview of salvation by grace. The Exodus is behind, the Promise Land is ahead. The Israelites murmur. Poisonous snakes were sent to punish. Many were ill and dying. Then God stepped in. Moses was told to put a "Brass Snake" on a pole. Anyone snake-bitten could look and live, *AMAZING!* The people had sinned; they were not deserving. There were no regulations to be kept. The people were simply told to come, look, and live. They did. They lived. The "Brass Snake" was a provision of grace. The mercy of God provided. Yet the healing was not universal! Only those that looked could live. God produced— the needy obeyed. This event gave a peek at grace—the love, mercy, and compassion of God. It required dependency from the needy—a trust in God. There could be no grounds for boasting. Healing was all to the glory of God. Those healed should have learned! To simply trust God . . . to praise God for His power . . . to profoundly thank God for His provision. But they did not.

The "Brass Snake" was a provision of grace—but it was not grace within itself. Jesus was/is grace! "And the Word was made flesh, and dwelt among us, (and we beheld his glory, the glory as of the only begotten of the Father,) free of grace and truth . . . For the law was given by Moses, but grace and truth came by Jesus Christ" (Jn. 1:14-17). The "Brass Snake" was provided by God. It came out of grace. But, personally, it cost God nothing. It was impersonal. Man was indebted— but not motivated. Christ is grace! Christ, personally, cost God everything. God is personally involved in Christ. This motivates! The price, cost, pain of Christ for us! *AMAZING GRACE!* Grace is the only permanent motivation in Christianity. "And I, if I be lifted up from the earth, will draw all men unto me. This he said, signifying what death he should die" (Jn. 12:32,33). This is the Gospel! The "Good News"! That man in sin can be saved in Christ! It is grace! Man in dependence obeys and lives. There is no place for human boasting. Jesus paid it all! Salvation is a finished product. Man responds to grace. We are saved by grace; don't you ever forget it!

Grace Is For Weakness

Man wants to be a winner. He gives up self-reliance lastly. Modern religious psychology paints "Christians as Winners." They do not fail; they are achievers; they live trouble-free lives. Sometimes it seems like "Can you top this?" Said devotees either know, have, or can do something superior to all others. It hits man at his pride to admit, accept grace. Man wishes to be strong—not weak. He refuses "to be on charity." Man is embarrassed to ask. *REMEMBER!* Christianity is for weak people! ". . . for I am not come to call the righteous, but sinners to repentance" (Mt. 9:13). "Come unto me, all ye that labour and are heavy laden, and I will give you rest" (Mt. 11:28). ". . . my grace is sufficient for thee: for my strength is made perfect in weakness. Most gladly therefore will I rather glory in my infirmities, that the power of Christ may rest upon me" (2 Cor. 12:9). *AMAZING GRACE!* Not for the elite, powerful, successful, rich, special . . . but for the weak ignorant, unwanted, despised people! The church is not a hotel for saints but a hospital for sinners. Jesus is the Savior of the sick, the suffering, the fear-filled.

One brother prayed, "Lord, forgive me of my sins." A scriptural prayer. But another had a deeper insight, "Lord, forgive me of my righteousness." He was saying man is so prone to revert back to human strength and reliance. In Jesus we do not receive what we earn. We receive something earned for us on the cross by Jesus (Rom. 3:24-26). Law confronts man at his own strength and demands the impossible; the Gospel reaches man at his weakness to accept God's strength.

A Righteousness Not Our Own

Man thinks he is saved with codes, rules, regulations, laws, "pat answers to all situations." This is the intrinsic pride of self-righteousness, and the area in which the conscience often operates—conscience not as a life guide but as a way of self-justification by which we defend, vindicate, and right ourselves. This is Phariseeism, legalism, orthodoxy. The problem of the law keeper is not that he doesn't keep the law well enough—he thinks he is saved by keeping it. Face it . . . most of us are legalists. We resist the agony of thought, honesty, and change. Abraham and Sarah tried to "go it alone." The result was Ishmael. All man can do is make Ishmaels! Heaven is not for those who think they are good—but for those who know they are bad.

Therefore, there must be a vicarious righteousness supplied. This, Jesus did, at the cross. "For he hath made him to be sin for us. Who knew no sin; that we might be made the righteousness of God in him" (2 Cor. 5:21). Jesus was perfect, sinless, without guile. He could not die for His sins! Therefore He died for ours! The saving grace of God comes not over, under, or around judgment but through righteousness and judgment. The judgment of the cross is the moral back bone of redemption. Grace is "no blue-eyed blond" . . . no cheap cop-out! Heaven gave its "Crown Jewel" for righteousness. When John Bunyan was asked, "Where is your righteousness?" he answered, "in heaven." Jesus is our righteousness. "But of him are ye in Christ Jesus, who of God is made unto us wisdom, and righteousness, and sanctification, and redemption" (1 Cor. 1:30). What Christ did magnified the law of God just as it had been prophesied. Grace is not merely amnesty! *JESUS PAID IT ALL!* One either accepts this and acts upon it—or one tries to mix Judaism and the Gospel—which is not gospel.

Justification is a legal concept. Time must be spent studying the atonement. What, really, is salvation? How can a "just God" justify the guilty? How can the guilty be pronounced "not guilty"? Christians are not merely "paroled"; they are pardoned. What is vicarious atonement, ransom (to whom paid?), expiation, propitiation, adoption, reconciliation? These are the basics; we must keep returning to the basics. "Justified" means judged righteous, not guilty, a verdict handed down by a judge. If you would make a word play, "Just-as-if-I-had-not-sinned." Sin cannot be "un-made" . . . sin cannot be fixed . . . the consequences of sin remain. But sin can be forgiven and sinners justified. This is provided by grace. The cross is God's answer. God was not "winking at sin" nor looking the other way. At the cross God dealt with the sin reality. Sinners can stand justified before God today only because Christ dealt with sin at the cross. This righteousness is already in Christ, and in Him alone! The Gospel does not focus upon sinners or believers, but upon Jesus. "For all have sinned and come short of the glory of God: Being justified freely by his grace through the redemption that is in Christ Jesus: Whom God hath set forth to be a propitiation through faith in his blood, to declare his righteousness for the remission of sins that are past, through the forbearance of God: To declare, I say, at this time his righteousness: that he might be just, and the justifier of him which believeth in Jesus. Where is boasting then? It is excluded. By what law? of works? Nay; but by the law of faith . . . Do we then make void the law through faith? God forbid: yea, we establish the law" (Rom. 3:23-31).

"For they being ignorant of God's righteousness and going about to establish their own righteousness, have not submitted themselves unto the righteousness of God. For Christ is the end of the law for righteousness to everyone that believeth" (Rom. 10:3,4). "And be found in him, not having mine own righteousness, which is of the law but that which is through the faith of Christ, the righteousness which is of God by faith: That I may know him, and the power of his resurrection, and the fellowship of his suffering, being made conformable unto his death'' (Phil. 3:9,10). ''Little children, let no man deceive you: he that doeth righteousness is righteous, even as he is righteous'' (1 Jn. 3:7).

''But not as the offence, so also is the free gift. For if through the offence of one many be dead, much more the grace of God, and the gift by grace, which is by one man, Jesus Christ, hath abounded unto many . . . For if by one man's offence death reigned by one; much more they which receive abundance of grace and of the gift of righteousness shall reign in life by one, Jesus Christ. Therefore as by the offence of one judgment came upon all men to condemnation; even so by the righteousness of one the free gift came upon all men unto justification of life . . . Moreover the law entered, that the offence might abound. But where sin abounded, grace did much more abound! That as sin hath reigned unto death, even so might grace reign through righteousness unto eternal life by Jesus Christ our Lord'' (Rom. 5:15-21). ''For if the ministration of condemnation be glory, much more doth the ministration of righteousness exceed in glory'' (2 Cor. 3:9). ''For he hath made him to be sin for us, who knew no sin; that we might be made the righteousness of God in him'' (2 Cor. 5:21). ''I don't frustrate the grace of God: for if righteousness came by the law, then Christ is dead in vain'' (Gal. 2:12).

''Is the law then against the promises of God? God forbid: for if there had been a law given which could have given life, verily righteousness should have been by the law'' (Gal. 3:21). ''Being filled with the fruits of righteousness, which are by Jesus Christ, unto the glory and praise of God'' (Phil. 1:11). From these scriptures it is evident that sinners are pronounced ''not guilty'' in Christ. This righteousness is available to all sinners—not one's record as a ''law keeper,'' but one's response to the gift of God's grace. How can a just God justify sinners? Through the redemption of Christ.

This allows the redeemed to ''treat people right.'' Phariseeism crushes people in the name of God! Legalists will maintain their regulations regardless what this does to people. The system must not become more important than people. ''. . . The sabbath was made for man, and not man for the sabbath; Therefore the Son of Man is Lord also of the sabbath" (Mk. 2:27,28). Grace received produces mercy. A mercy problem is actually a grace problem. One who will not accept grace cannot give mercy. The person of Jesus and the saving love of God produce ethics that are people-centered. When regulations are central then Phariseeism is substituted for Christianity. Pharisees cannot grasp the depths of the love of God. Like the Jews of old Pharisees "stumble" over the cross. They do not need the grace of God nor want the God of grace. Being law-centered rather than grace-centered they cannot have assurance, joy, and peace. Legalists proselytize rather than evangelize. To proselytize means to change people to our religion, to conform to our ideas and opinions, and to make them disciples after our own likeness. To evangelize is to preach Christ—the Gospel—the grace—the gift of God! Evangelism is bringing men to Jesus!

The Law And The Gospel

The understanding of "law and Gospel" remains illusive! So many cannot grasp the distinction. There is grace in the Law and grace is not lawless. The subtle temptation is to make Christianity a "spruced-up Law of Moses." Several things must be understood:

(1) As systems, grace and law contradict each other. The key word is "system." If man can do it then grace is not needed. But man cannot do it—therefore he needs grace. Man's salvation was achieved apart from the Law (Rom. 3:21-26); for if salvation can be accomplished through man's own works of merit, then grace is no more grace, "And if by grace, then is it no more of works: otherwise grace is no more grace. But if it be of works, then is it no more grace: otherwise work is no more work" (Rom. 11:6). Either man is innocent and does not need saving or man saves himself in perfection. Man is neither innocent nor perfect! One who has no sin has no need of grace. Justification by works is on the grounds of innocence not forgiveness. But man in sin requires grace. When one violates the law then the law condemns! This is the way law works. Law cannot use grace! When one violates the law he not only loses the blessing that could have come in keeping

96

the law he also receives the penalty for violating it. Therefore violation of law renders one "speechless." There is nothing man can say or do! By the law is the knowledge of sin (Rom. 3:20), the exceeding sinfulness of sin (Rom. 7:6-17). "For whosoever shall keep the whole law, and yet offend in one point, he is guilty of all" (James 2:10). Any retreat to law is a denial of grace. The law principle cannot house the grace principle. Grace and law are mutually exclusive.

(2) Grace does not reject law. Grace is not "anti-law" (antinomianism). A road has two ditches on either side. A careening car trying to avoid one ditch usually crashes into the other. People tend to go from "all law" to "no law." "All law" is wrong, wrong, wrong! "No law" is wrong, wrong, wrong! Because one is not under law does not mean one is without law. The Jews made the Law their "Christ"; Christ is our law!

You cannot abolish legalism by abolishing laws! Legalism is not synonymous with law. Legalism is faith in your ability to keep law. You cannot abolish legalism by making more laws. Someone observed man has made a zillion laws trying to enforce "The Ten Commands." Law forces more law.

One cannot appreciate grace unless one understands the law. ". . . for ye are not under the law, but under grace. What then? Shall we sin, because we are not under the law, but under grace? God forbid" (Rom. 6:14,15). Another paradox . . . the law was established by being abolished (Col. 2:12-17). Familiar scripture must be read more closely. The Law is not dead— we are dead to the Law. "Wherefore, my brethren, ye also are become dead to the law by the body of Christ; that ye should be married to another" (Rom. 7:4).

(3) Christians are under grace not law. The temptation is to think that grace is necessary for salvation, then law for living. Christianity is not the "Top Story" in Judaism. Man is not left upon his own resources. The part of the Law the Jews thought they did best is gone! The child of God remains dependent upon God's grace daily, continually. Christianity is a life of grace.

Neither the alien sinner nor the child of God can be righteous on the ground of works.

Do not fear grace! Read Romans 6. Paul concludes, "We are not free to sin but free to serve." "But God be thanked, that ye were the servants of sin, but ye have obeyed from the heart that form of doctrine which was delivered you. Being then made free from sin, ye become the servants of righteousness" (Rom. 6:17,18). Meet me in heaven.

Questions

1. Discuss the "Brass Snake" as it illustrates grace in Christ.
2. Are Christians winners? Do you wish to be weak? Does self die hard? What did Paul say about this?
3. Discuss imputed righteousness.
4. Discuss atonement, justification, ransom, salvation, sanctification, propitiation, expiation. Have we neglected these fundamentals? Who is our righteousness?
5. Discuss law and grace. How are law-systems and grace-systems incompatible? Are we better at law or grace? Do we fear grace as much as law?

"Grace And Peace"

Introduction

AMAZING GRACE! Tell men what God did before you tell men what to do. Grace is infinitely larger than we imagine or allow. "Every good and every perfect gift is from above, and cometh down from the Father of lights, with whom is no variableness, neither shadow of turning" (James 1:17). God not only "is"—"God is good" (Psa. 100:3-5). We are so accustomed hearing the Bible preached negatively that when a little bit of good news comes out we tend to reject it thinking, "Naw, God couldn't be that good!" There can be many scriptures used without any Gospel (Good News) presented. The Great Commission focuses upon "Gospel" not creed! The subtle tendency is to grow in knowledge, doctrine, methods, and organization without growing in Christ. *CHRIST— CHRIST—CHRIST!* Learn to say Christ without mumbling. Realism without love results in cynicism. Too much "church work" is, in reality, cynicism. Do not try to manipulate people. Love people and use things; do not love things and use people.

One may be wrong about some things but he cannot be wrong about grace. Christianity is grace at its beginning, grace in its continuance, and grace at its end. Grace is the work of God from beginning to end. To God be the glory. Salvation is by grace (1 Pet. 1:10). God elected us before we accepted Him (1 Pet. 1:2). Since we have tasted that the Lord is gracious we are not afraid of anything He purposes for us (1 Pet. 2:3). God's grace is manifold (1 Pet. 4:10). Christians stand in grace (1 Pet. 5:12). God is the God of all grace (1 Pet. 5:10). Whatever begins and continues with grace will always lead to God's glory (1 Pet. 5:10). Believers are kept by the power of

God (1 Pet. 1:5). It is high time God's people give grace the priority it deserves. Too often our zeal promotes our works without founding our works in grace. Sometimes grace is barely mentioned or "explained away." Grace must never become secondary in Christian experience.

Your writer was an only child reared on a cotton farm. My parents worked to provide this farm—for me. Without me, the farm was meaningless. "To an inheritance incorruptible, and undefiled, and that fadeth not away, reserved in heaven for you" (1 Pet. 1:4). Most can believe that God is preparing heaven for us, but few have grasped that, equally so, God is preparing us for the inheritance. Without God, there is no heaven; without us, heaven has no meaning. Every morning upon awakening I remind myself of two things (1) God loves me. (2) Jesus died for me. This is the permanent motivation of grace. I am His and He is mine. We are saved by grace—don't you ever forget it!

Grace And Peace

Paul opened and closed each epistle with the words, "Grace and Peace." Rom. 1:5,7; 16:20,24; 1 Cor. 1:3,4; 15:23; 2 Cor. 1:2; 13:14; Gal. 1:3; 6;16,18; Eph. 1:2; 6:23,24; Phil. 1:2; 4:23; Col. 1:2; 4:18; 1 Thess. 1:1; 5:28; 2 Thess. 1:2; 3:18; 1 Tim. 1:2; 6:21; 2 Tim. 1:2; 4:22; Tit. 1:4; 3:15. Paul's two favorite words were grace and peace. Peter also practiced this, 1 Pet. 1:2; 5:14; 2 Pet. 1:2; 3:18. It is evident from the unanimity of said usages that grace and peace are vital.

It would be foolish to deny said words were a salutation and benediction. God edits severely; His Bible does not waste words. Yet God allows personal feelings with writers and readers. Read Romans 16! God allowed Paul to reminisce. Salutations and benedictions are necessary. However, these words must not be reduced only to salutations and benedictions. Commentaries skip over these verses. Few comments are made. These two words "must say it all." They are too uniform to be lightly dismissed! Paul and Peter were not merely saying "hello" and "goodbye." This was their emphasis—grace and peace! This must be ours, too! When one stands in the grace of God he has the peace of God! Grace produces peace. Grace enables; peace results. This is the evaluation of both Christians and Churches. Build upon grace and you have peace. Grace and peace are the significant words in Christianity. The great spiritual principle is that the surest way to increase one's faith in God is to concentrate one's attention upon the utter faithfulness of God! We must become increasingly aware that it is not *"Who"* we are that counts, but rather *"whose"* we are! It is one thing to seek the will of God. It is another thing to think one can do it under human power! This statement is crucial. One is not left upon his own resources. God's will can only be done under God's power. God not only reveals His will—He supplies the power! "Grace and Peace."

Grace

Paul and Peter both zeroed in on grace! This must be the soil for our entire Christian experience! Grace covered our sins. Grace is greater than all our sins. "But not as the offense, so also is the free gift. For if through the offence of one many be dead, much more the grace of God, and the gift of grace, which is by one man, Jesus Christ, hath abounded unto many . . . much more they which receive abundance of grace and of the gift of righteousness shall reign in life by one, Jesus Christ . . . But where sin abounded, grace did much more abound: That as sin hath reigned unto death, even so might grace reign through righteousness unto eternal life by Jesus Christ our Lord" (Rom. 5:12-21). "But we believe that we shall be saved through the grace of the Lord Jesus, in like manner as they" (Acts 15:11). "Concerning which salvation the prophets sought and searched diligently, who prophesied of the grace which should come unto you" (1 Pet. 1:10). "Being justified freely by his grace through the redemption that is in Christ Jesus" (Rom. 3:24). "Being therefore justified by faith, we have peace with God through our Lord Jesus Christ; through whom also we have had our access by faith unto this grace wherein we stand; and we rejoice in hope of the glory of God" (Rom. 5:1,2).

To say "hello" and "goodbye" with the word "grace" is

to remind ourselves of our glorious salvation in Christ. We are reminded who we belong to! Christians must study the atonement—how God saved sinners. Our heads "split at the thought" of God's incarnation in man . . . how could a death at Calvary remit my sins? We must dig deeper into grace. The idea that God "ransomed sinners from Satan" is blasphemy. Man did sin from temptation by Satan. But man has never been owned by Satan. Although there is vicarious substitution in Christ atonement is far deeper than satisfying law. God is God. Law reveals God. But God is not at the mercy of any of His attributes let alone law. Law is not God! Human minds and human words cannot grasp the profound meaning of salvation by grace. God did not merely stand by as a spectator at the cross, in childish anger, demanding restitution for a broken law or an offended honor. 2 Cor. 5:19-21 has God in Christ reconciling the world back to God. Notice what is not taught— Christ was not in man reconciling God to the world. God, in Christ, stepped into our helpless, damned condition to take all the penalties of sin upon Himself, gathering all our sins into His great heart and consuming them in the fires of His own love. This lifts Christianity from a mechanical "business transaction" into a profoundly personal love. This is the meaning of "grace." Say it! Believe it! Live it!

Peace

Grace and peace must never become "trite." The deepest and the most universal desire of the human heart is peace. Our cry has always been, "peace." One who stands in the grace of God has the peace of God. Peace cannot be built, earned, attained by men. Peace is the result of grace! "These things I have spoken unto you, that in me ye might have peace" (Jn. 16:33). "For he is our peace, who hath made both one . . . for to make in himself of twain one new man, so making peace" (Eph. 2:14-16). The fruit of the Spirit is peace (Gal. 5:22,23). "And the peace of God, which passes all understanding, shall keep your hearts and minds through Jesus Christ" (Phil. 4:4-7). "And let the peace of God rule in your hearts" (Col. 3:15). "And the fruit of righteousness is sown in peace of them that make peace" (James 3:18). *PEACE!* What a word! Over 400 times in the Bible—88 times in the New Testament. *SHALOM!* Good bye (God be with you)!

Peace is totality, wholeness, balance. Peace is from God and not man. It is given not earned; it is received not attained. It is the peace that comes in Christ knowing that one is safe in what He has done. Men look for peace everywhere but where it is—in Jesus! Grace is what God did—Peace is the result.

Peace is far greater than the thoughts of men. Peace is not in man, in treaties, in the absence of war. Men talk peace while planning war. Men keep on signing peace treaties not worth the paper written on. Peace is not based upon the fear of war but the love of peace. Men must desire a "land of peace" not a "piece of the land." Peace is a state of heart, mind. Men cannot have the "Peace of God" without having the "God of Peace." Men claim a desire for peace yet what they wish is gained only by war! Peace is not what a man has/has not. Peace is who a man is—internal versus external. "Flee also youthful lusts: but follow righteousness, faith, charity, peace, with them that call on the Lord out of a pure heart" (2 Tim. 2:22). "Ye lust, and have not: ye kill, and desire to have, and cannot obtain: ye fight and war, yet ye have not, because ye ask not. Ye ask, and receive not, because ye ask amiss, that ye may consume it upon your lusts" (James 4:1-3).

Peace comes from righteousness. A thought! We pray often for peace yet seldom for righteousness. Righteousness is "rightness"—with God, self, and others. Men try to have peace without change—without holiness or purity. Peace does not come with nations or congregations. Peace is personal—within hearts. Jesus talked about the pure in heart before He blessed the peacemakers (Mt. 5:8-12). Jesus did not discuss "peace-lovers" or "peace-helpers" . . . He talked about "peace makers." Peace involves a cost, price, sacrifice. Wrong persons cannot produce peace. Righteousness is sown in peace with those who make peace, "For unto us a child is born, unto us a son is given: and the government shall be upon his shoulder: and his name shall be called wonderful, counsellor, the mighty God, the everlasting Father, the Prince of Peace" (Isa. 9:6). "And your feet shod with the preparation of the gospel of peace" (Eph. 6:15). Peace is possible to the degree one grows in grace (2 Pet. 3:18).

Jesus Stands And Knocks

"Behold, I stand at the door, and knock: if any man hear my voice, and open the door, I will come in to him, and will sup with him, and he with me" (Rev. 3:20). Grace . . . righteousness . . . peace. Notice the "humility of God." God will not coerce—ever brethren. He came and died for us. He invites all to come. "And the spirit and the bride say, come, and let him that heareth say, come, and let him that is athirst come. And whosoever will, let him take of the water of life freely" (Rev. 22:17). All are invited yet none are pressured. Whosoever will may come; whosoever will may go! Ever God's profound power will not disrespect the free moral agency of man. *AMAZING GRACE!* A God who deserves, gave, and continues to give—can be rejected! The key to the lock is on the inside—within our hearts. Receive grace! Open the door and make Jesus the Lord of your life.

Luke Is Re-Visited

Your writer authored *Will God Run?* twenty years ago. It has been his desire since to study and write about grace. "And he arose, and came to his father. But when he was yet a great way off, his father saw him, and had compassion, and ran, and fell on his neck, and kissed him" (Luke 15:20). Luke 15 is grace preached by Jesus! The greatest sermon ever heard on grace. The Father *"ran"* to meet the Prodigal; He also *"walked"* to talk with the Elder son! *GRACE!* The Pharisees rebelled with grace! Jesus said three things about the Prodigal?

(1) I want my way (verses 12,13). This is sin. The lust of man rather than the peace of God. M. D. Anderson is a great hospital in Houston. Yet so many patients there die! They go only when cancer is in an advanced state—when hope is practically nil. When cancer is treated early there is hope. The same with man. Men covet, lust, fantasize! James says that matured lust results in sin and sin results in death (James 1). The problem lies within the heart! Man must protect his heart. "Casting down imaginations, and every high thing that exalteth itself against the knowledge of God, and bringing into captivity

104

every thought to the obedience of Christ" (2 Cor. 10:5). The plight of man—he *wants* his way.

(2) I want (verses 14-17). Satan promises but cannot deliver. The exciting ads do not live up to their promise. Satan never shows the pain and loss in sin. Broken lives, homes, hearts. The wages of sin is death. Satan only destroys. Sin ravages. Man pays a high price "to do his own thing."

(3) I am wanted (verses 20-24). The Prodigal came to himself. Yet salvation is still mechanical—a "business transaction." He did not come seeking grace—he would have been happy only with a job! *AMAZING GRACE!* The Father ran, fell on his neck, and kissed him! *GRACE!* The Prodigal received grace. The Elder Son was enraged with grace. Grace and peace.

The Surprises In Judgment

The judgment is coming. One day we will stand before the bar on high. Someone suggested heaven will have three surprises: (1) We will miss some we thought would we there. Man judges outward appearance; God looks upon the heart. All man can evaluate is the outward! Some considered faithful are not. The Rich Young Ruler will not be there. The Pharisees will not be there. Zealots who trust themselves rather than Christ will not be there. (2) Some will be there we did not expect. Rahab the harlot . . . the sinner in Luke 18 . . . Matthew 21:31. Those in heaven are those who accepted, trusted, and lived in grace. (3) We are there. We know our needs, mistakes, sins. We all have closets crammed full with skeletons. There is no way we can make heaven . . . except by grace. Trusting not merely trying. Those there are there by grace. Meet me in heaven.

Grace And Peace

When I stand before the throne,
Dressed in beauty not my own:
When I see Thee as Thou art,
Love Thee with unsinning heart:
Then, Lord, shall I fully know—
Not till then—how much I owe!

105

Questions

1. Review our focus upon grace. Focus upon Christ.
2. What are Paul's two favorite words? Are they merely words of politeness or do they "say it all"? Does Peter agree with Paul? Do you usually skip over salutations and benedictions?
3. Discuss the Hebrew word, shalom.
4. Discuss atonement.
5. Do we really want peace? Are we willing to pay its price? Discuss how man fails in his pursuit of peace.
6. Discuss Revelation 3:17-20.
7. Discuss Luke 15.
8. Will *you* be surprised in the judgment?

Printed in the United States
218826BV00003B/2/P

9 780890 980323